Lewis & Clark

Across the Northwest

A REGIONAL GUIDE
Washington ■ **Idaho** ■ **Oregon**

CHERYLL HALSEY

hancock house

ISBN 0-88839-560-4

Cataloging in Publication Data

Halsey, Cheryll
    Lewis & Clark across the Northwest : a regional guide :
Washington, Idaho, Oregon / Cheryll Halsey.

Includes bibliographical references and index.
ISBN 0-88939-560-8

    1. Lewis and Clark Expedition (1804–1806). 2. Northwest,
Pacific—Discovery and exploration. 3. Northwest, Pacific—
Description and travel. I. Title. II. Title: Lewis and Clark across
the Northwest.

F592.7.H338 2006   917.9504'2   C2005-906691-1

Printed in Indonesia — TK Printing

Editing: Nancy Miller
Production: Ingrid Luters
Photos and illustrations by Cheryll Halsey unless otherwise credited.

Published simultaneously in Canada and the United States by

HANCOCK HOUSE PUBLISHERS LTD.
19313 Zero Avenue, Surrey, B.C. Canada V3S 9R9
(604) 538-1114 Fax (604) 538-2262

HANCOCK HOUSE PUBLISHERS
1431 Harrison Avenue, Blaine, WA U.S.A. 98230-5005
(604) 538-1114 Fax (604) 538-2262

Website: www.hancockhouse.com
Email: sales@hancockhouse.com

Contents

Acknowledgments

This book is a direct result of the influence and support of Robert R. Beale, Pomeroy, Washington, a historian and farmer who approached people, life and the environment with high regard and respect. Some of the photographs in this book are from his collection. He took the time to nurture a friendship with Nez Perce elders and to record oral histories. Albert Moore, a Nez Perce elder, told him the story of Wetxuiis and Lewis and Clark, which is contained in this book. Robert also gathered important information on the Three Forks Indian Trail in Garfield County and was a member of the Washington State Governor's Commission for the Lewis and Clark Trail. I worked with Robert Beale for several years in researching and writing another book on the horse-farming era of the Pacific Northwest. My gratitude to him and to the forces that be.

Miles Graham Smith, my favorite muse, actually sang as he fine-tuned maps on the computer: "Serve God, love me and heal" [Shakespeare].

Lewis and Clark Trail Heritage Foundation continues to inspire and inform. The Washington State Deptartment of Parks and Recreation has assisted and given permission for reproduction of their maps. Our thanks. Accolades to others who have encouraged and supported me in this effort with reading, suggestions, computer support and savvy; they have all been much appreciated. Specific thanks to Linda Jordan, Michael Eichner and Sophie Horst. And, always, love and thanks to my family for patience and understanding. I can't leave out Avi and Yin for unflagging, nonverbal support as I worked into the wee hours; they were always there, though snoozing.

> In memory of Robert R. Beale
> *"When you allow me to share you have gifted me.*
> *Pass it on and our giving will be multiplied."*

How to Use This Book

The chapters in this book are organized to represent different segments of the route followed by the Corps of Discovery across Idaho, Washington and Oregon. Each leg of the journey had a certain quality of experience to it. **The first chapter** describes their crossing of the Continental Divide—three times on the way west— as they looked for the most practical route. This was the most grueling terrain they encountered on the entire trip and it was their introduction to the northwest. At this point they met with Shoshone Indians to trade for horses and found that Sacagawea, the young wife of their French interpreter, was a sister to the chief. She had been captured as a young girl and now returned home as a member of the expedition.

Chapter two describes another dramatic event involving an Indian woman, the Nez Perce Wetxuiis, who was never mentioned in the journals of the expedition, but who may have saved the lives of the starving and exhausted white men. The Nez Perce proved to be stalwart friends who shared food, knowledge of the country, and dugout canoe construction so the Corps could continue on toward the ocean.

Chapter three focuses on reaching the Columbia River, the Big River, a critical milestone that they hoped would take them swiftly and easily to the Pacific. They met more friendly tribes there and joined them in feasts of salmon. William Clark recorded a recipe for salmon, Indian style, in his journal.

Chapter four describes the explorers' encounter with the Chinookan Traders at Celilo Falls, the Great Falls of the Columbia, where they entered yet another world in the culture of Northwest Indians. Here they were faced with the sophisticated center of trade for the Pacific Plateau Trade System. Tribes from downriver came to trade and to meet with those from the eastern plateau region of the northwest. The Corps entered the spectacular Columbia River

Gorge, navigated dangerous rapids in dugout canoes, and survived to continue onward downstream.

Chapter five covers a grueling 150 miles downstream from the beginning of tidal influence to the Pacific Ocean. Battered by storms and tides, this relatively short distance was anything but a downstream float trip. However, they did plant the flag for the United States on the northern shore of the Columbia River, near the ocean, and thus staked a claim to the northwest. This done, they immediately made plans to pass the winter in a sheltered spot on the south shore and made their way across the river to build a stockade they called Fort Clatsop. The winter passed there is covered in **chapter six**. They brought journals and maps up to date, hunted, made moccasins, and traded with their Indian neighbors. It rained nearly every day they were at Fort Clatsop until they left for the return journey on March 18, 1806.

Chapter seven is an account of their homeward journey east— now up the Columbia. They portaged around rapids and, finally, took an overland route to the lands of the Nez Perces. **Chapter eight** describes their reunion with their Indian friends and their stay with them while waiting for the snow to melt enough to open Lolo Pass for their last crossing of the Continental Divide.

This book ends with an epilogue and brief profiles of Captains Lewis and Clark, the Shoshone woman Sacagawea, and York, Clark's slave.

Each chapter contains a trail guide which points out actual sites of camps and significant events and landmarks experienced during the expedition. There are also regional places of interest and sightseeing opportunities listed, along with maps.

One of the directives given to the Captains was to collect information on flora and fauna that might be new to science. They did so with great scientific care and skill. At the end of this book you will find a description of the plants and animals the explorers catalogued as they traveled across the northwest.

This book can be used in either of two ways or in combination. First, it can be used as a historical and regional guide for following the path of the Lewis and Clark Expedition across present-day Washington, Oregon and Idaho, from Lolo Pass in the Bitterroot Mountains to the mouth of the Columbia River at the Pacific Ocean. Enough of the trail is accessible by car, hiking or bicycling for an opportunity to imagine ourselves in the moccasins of the explorers. Alternatively, the book is a useful guide for shorter trips around the region.

The ethnographic and natural history of the area, as it was then and as it is now, remains a rich and important aspect of the Pacific Northwest. It is my hope that this book will enhance that experience and awareness for the reader and encourage further reading and interest in the subjects presented here.

Trail Stewardship

As you travel in the footsteps of the Lewis and Clark Trail Expedition and the homelands of the Native peoples along the trail:

- Leave no trace—help protect the environment
- Respect private property—don't trespass
- Protect archeological resources—leave things where you find them
- Help ensure that the Lewis and Clark Trail experience is still here 200 years from now!

Take notice of the country you pass through, it's [*sic*] general face, soil, river, mountains, it's [*sic*] productions animal, vegetable, & mineral so far as they may be new to us & also be useful; the latitudes of places...; the names, numbers, & dwellings of the inhabitants, and such particularities as you can learn of them.

— PRESIDENT THOMAS JEFFERSON
April 30, 1793.

Preface

Meriwether Lewis and William Clark have always been the quintessential rugged individuals of America for me. The mountains of Idaho, called "terrible" by the explorers, were my own mountains. Stories of the rugged terrain, cougars and Indians whetted my appetite to trek off into the unknown when I was a youngster. This trekking took place, for the most part, in my imagination. This book is for all of us who imagine and are not likely to trek in the manner of the Lewis and Clark. It is possible to drive much of the trail, even the backcountry Lolo Trail if you have a permit and a four-wheel drive.

These explorers did just that; they explored. They proceeded on to the Pacific and back again to St. Louis, Missouri in a time when the United States was still young. Thomas Jefferson had just made the Louisiana Purchase of 1803 and wanted to know what he had bought. He sent the Corps of Discovery out west to have a look and to report back on all sorts of scientific things, like the plants, animals, rivers and mountains. He wanted maps and reports on Indian tribes and, more than anything, a navigable trade route to the Pacific.

You will have a richer experience if you will stand where they stood and imagine the grandeur and vastness of the northwest they experienced. Contrast their experience with our current-day experience. Journey with Lewis and Clark in your mind. Stop to rest or camp or hike. Look more closely at the plants, birds, and animals you encounter. Wonder how the Columbia could once have been so full of migrating salmon that it seemed that only fins, crowded together, protruded from the water.

Seeing the present through the eyes and ears of history gives us the opportunity to note and evaluate the changes that have come in 200 years. Preservation of cultural and historic sites, as well as species and terrain, is our task now. Let us remember the courage and purpose of the Corps of Discovery and make it ours as well. I hope this book invites a reverence for the place and, like the explorers, that you be awed by it.

Introduction

Captains Meriwether Lewis and William Clark faithfully recorded
their observations and experiences as they crossed lands occupied
by Shahaptian-speaking Natives of Idaho and along the Columbia
River territories of the Chinookan- and Salish-speaking tribes. Personal journals were kept by Sergeants Floyd, Gass and Ordway as
well as Private Whitehouse. We have all these accounts, written during 1805 and 1806 to draw on today.

There is another, unwritten, account of what took place between
the explorers and the Shahaptian, Chinookan, Salish and Coastal
tribes. That story is from the oral history of the Natives themselves.
For example, the Nez Perce tribal history of when Lewis and Clark
first came to the Nez Perce at the camas gathering grounds in Idaho
is very specific. It tells what happened from their perspective. The
journals of the expedition tell what happened from the explorer's
perspective. It is important to respect and consider both.

The Shahaptian tribes of 1805 inhabited the area along the
waters of the Columbia and its tributaries from the Cascade Range
on the west to the Bitterroot Mountains on the east, and from about
46°N to 44°S. The relationship of the linguistically related tribes is
that of a large family.

Lewis and Clark first encountered the Nez Perce, the largest
group of the collective tribes, when they emerged from the snow-
covered Bitterroot Mountains, starving and exhausted—a dramatic
moment for all. They were met with hospitable gestures and the
Indians willingly shared their small stores of food.

Meetings with the Chinookan- and Salish-speaking people of
the Lower Columbia and on to the Pacific were experienced differ-
ently by the members of the expedition. There was an established
trade system in place along the Columbia River and the bearded
white men who came downriver in dugout canoes were less than
welcome in the marketplace of the river. There were instances of
theft and threats and, on the return trip, Captain Lewis' temper

flared to a point where he threatened to shoot an Indian. The Chinooks collected a tribute, almost a toll, for passing through their river territory. They expected respect. They took items for payment when the expedition corp neglected the cultural norms. The contrast was not in the innate superiority of one group over another, but rather in the perception of the "other" in a time, place and circumstance much different, both for the explorers and for the Indians. The mountain tribes needed friends with guns because they were threatened by enemies with guns. The river tribes had good control of trading as middlemen on the river and the whites coming downriver could have been a threat to their status.

We are all human, not different from each other but rather uniquely and culturally diverse. All are ingenious in our own way. The Corps of Discovery undertook a journey of hardship into an unknown territory where they scientifically recorded and mapped. The journals that resulted are larger than the bible. Yet in spite of their ability and intelligence, when they came out of the Bitterroot Mountains to the Camas Prairie of Idaho they were starving. The Nez Perce Indians fed them and wondered why they starved when mosses used for famine food hung from the trees. Natives lived a culturally rich life here in the midst of routine hardship and were concerned that the white men might be stupid.

The journey from St. Louis to the Pacific and back again took 863 days. They began with fascination of a new world awaiting them with strange animals and wild people. For a year previous to leaving on the journey Lewis trained with a botanist at the direction of the scientifically minded President Thomas Jefferson. Lewis was a keen observer of plants and animals and Clark, particularly, was an excellent cartographer. The Pacific Northwest offered experiences of mountains, rivers, people, plants and animals that had never been recorded before. The new discoveries made by Lewis and Clark are noted in this book.

The Mission

In 1803 President Thomas Jefferson commissioned Meriwether Lewis and William Clark to find "the most direct and practicable water communication across the continent, for the purposes of commerce." They were directed to gather information relating to Native people encountered, terrain, plants and animals. The thinly disguised mission of the "Corps of Volunteers of North Western Discovery" was to obtain more than just scientific knowledge. The undisclosed purpose of the expedition was to strengthen American claims to the Columbia River drainage by making a transcontinental journey to its mouth on the Pacific Ocean.

The Situation

"We...[are] about to penetrate a country at least 2,000 miles in width, on which the foot of civilized man...[has] never trodden." So wrote Meriwether Lewis in his journal on April 7, 1805. The Corps of Discovery was preparing to leave a comfortable winter camp at Fort Mandan for the unknown of the northwest. They were to discover many things, one being that the influence of Euro-Americans had preceded them.

As they later crossed the Continental Divide they were indeed the first whites to cross this section of the Rocky Mountains. It would seem that Lewis and Clark might have expected to descend the Columbia and make their way to the Pacific through an untouched world where people lived as they had since time immemorial. In fact, the Native Indians of the Columbia Plateau had already experienced indirect white contact and the ensuing disruption to their way of life. For nearly a century they had been introduced to horses, disease of epidemic proportions and Euro-American trade goods. Trade and political alliances were influenced and adaptations had been made. When Lewis and Clark arrived Plateau Indians were eager for contacts and for opportunity to obtain weapons. They sorely needed to be able to defend themselves against tribes who had already obtained guns.

As the explorers traded and negotiated their way across the northwest they found friends, generosity, curiosity and occasional petty thievery. They found virtually no enemies.

Members of the Expedition

Officers: Meriwether Lewis and William Clark

Sergeants: Charles Floyd, Patrick Gass, John Ordway and

Nathaniel Pryor. Sergeant Floyd died on the Missouri, August 20, 1804, probably from a ruptured appendix.

Privates: William Bratton, John Collins, John Colter, Pierre Cruzatte, Joseph Field, Reuben Field, Robert Frazer, George Gibson, Silas Goodrich, Hugh Hall, Thomas Proctor Howard, Francois Labiche, Baptiste Lepage, Hugh McNeal, John Potts, George Shannon, John Shields, John B. Thompson, William Werner, Joseph Whitehouse, Alexander Willard, Richard Windsor and Peter Wiser

Interpreters: George Drouillard and Toussaint Charbonneau

Others: Sacagawea, Jean-Baptiste Charbonneau (infant) and York (Lewis' black slave). Seaman the dog also accompanied the group.

Summary to Accompany Maps

Leaving St. Louis on May 14, 1804, the expedition followed the Missouri River system for more than 1,000 miles and finally crossed the Continental Divide at Lemhi Pass in Idaho on August 12, 1805. Lemhi Pass is on the present-day border of Idaho and Montana; by crossing the Continental Divide they left the confines of the Louisiana Purchase. [The Lewis and Clark Backcountry Byway, a secondary road entirely in Idaho, can be accessed from Highway 28 at Tendoy, Idaho.]

At the divide, the waters flowed westward and they knew they were in the Columbia River system. Hoping for a water route to the Pacific, the expedition attempted to follow the Salmon River but found this route impossible. They were told by Shoshone Indians of a land trail to the west. They then went north over Lost Trail Pass and into the Bitterroot Valley and then west to the Nez Perce "Road to the Buffalo" over Lolo Pass. On September 9, 1805, they camped near the present town of Lolo Mt., at a site they called "Traveler's Rest."

A forced march across the snow-packed Bitterroot Mountains brought them to the land of the Nez Perce along the drainage of the Clearwater River. Those waters, ultimately, would reach the Pacific, the goal of the expedition.

The explorers traveled west to the Pacific and then back again across the northwest. The river voyage down the Columbia from the mouth of the Walla Walla River was the same traveling in both directions. The dates of the journey can be remembered easily. They traveled westward to the ocean in 1805 and eastward on the way home in 1806.

On the return trip they took an overland route to the mouth of the Clearwater River, since to proceed up the Snake River would have been impossible. Detailed maps throughout the book will aid in understanding the route.

PACIFIC OCEAN

WASHINGTON

100 mile scale

MTS.

Mt. St. Helens   Mt. Adams

Cascades

HayleyBay
&grays Bay

(The Dalles)
Cattle Falls

Columbia

COAST RANGES

Sauvie

Multnomah R.
(Willamette R.)

Mt. Hood

CASCADE

Deschutes R.

John Day R.

ORE

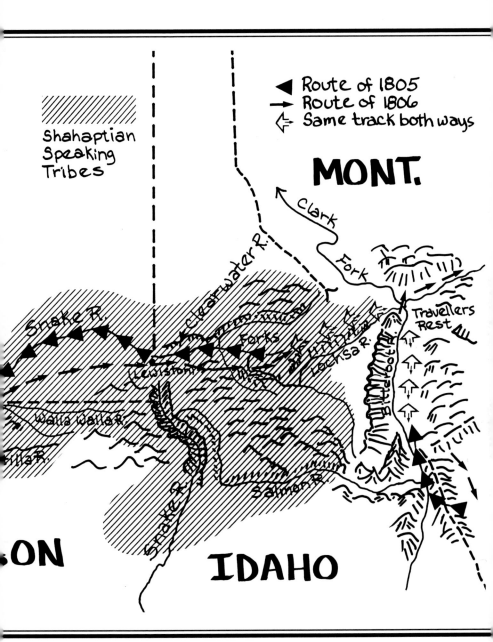

The route, forward and back of the Lewis and Clark Expedition of 1805–1806.
The shaded area indicates the lands occupied by Shahaptian-speaking native tribes.

CHAPTER 1

From Crossing the Continental Divide to the Land of the Nez Perce

■ August 12, 1805 ■

In August, 1805, the Corps of Discovery approached the headwaters of the Missouri River and the Rocky Mountains in western Montana. They had followed the river system for more than 1,000 miles and now entered a country about which they had no information. They knew they would need horses to pass over the mountains and hoped to obtain them from Sacagawea's people, the Lemhi Shoshone. Touissant Charbonneau had been hired by the expedition as an interpreter and it was hoped his Shoshone wife, the teenage Sacagawea, would be able to interpret and facilitate the trades for horses.

Captain Lewis, Drouillard, McNeal and Shields left the main party at Three Forks of the Beaverhead in present-day Montana and finally crossed the Continental Divide at Lemhi Pass on August 12, 1805. At that point the waters flowed westward and they realized they were in the Columbia River system. They were then in present-day Idaho, which is defined on the east by the Continental Divide.

They were searching for the Shoshone and hoping to trade for horses and get information about the country ahead. They didn't realize that most of the tribe was fishing in the lower valleys and would not return to the mountains for another month; however, they came upon three women digging for wild carrots. The women were terrified and were only calmed when Lewis took the older woman's hand and gave her gifts and then daubed vermilion on her face. Fortunately, Sacagawea had told him this was a sign of peace. The woman then led them toward the village. Suddenly, mounted warriors appeared and only after talking with the woman did they dismount and greet the small party. The chief was Cameahwait, who warmly embraced a surprised Lewis in what the captain called the "national hug."

Lewis set about trade negotiations over the next few days, surely with a sense of urgency since they had come as far as possible upriver and now needed to portage across the mountains. Cameahwait, too, discussed trade with a sense of need. His people needed trade goods, especially guns and ammunition, to protect themselves against enemies to the south and east who had superior weapons.

At this point Lewis lied to Cameahwait to ensure the Corps would have the needed horses to continue their journey. He told the chief that Americans who would come in the future would supply guns if the Shoshone provided furs. Later, at separate times, both he and Clark repeated this assurance.

Lewis' advance party and an entourage of Lemhi Shoshone then re-crossed the Continental Divide to the forks of the Beaverhead River to meet Clark. Clark wasn't there. Lewis had told Cameahwait that the others would be there and suspicions of the Indians began to rise. As fortune would have it Clark and the main party, including Sacagawea, appeared at just the right moment. Lewis named the place Camp Fortunate.

Sacagawea began to dance for joy as she recognized her brother, Chief Cameahwait. Several years before Sacagawea and another woman had been captured in a Hidatsa raid. Sacagawea now returned to the Lemhi Shoshone as the wife of Charbonneau, interpreter to the Corps. Imagine the emotion she felt, a lost child returned home. Through her sobbing Sacagawea was able to reassure her people that the Americans were to be trusted. She asked her tribe for their cooperation. There was much to tell each other as she spent time with her family and with her friend who had also been captured but had found her way home. Sacagawea had a baby to show her people, too. Her son Baptiste Charbonneau was still being carried in a cradleboard.

& Clark in Idaho

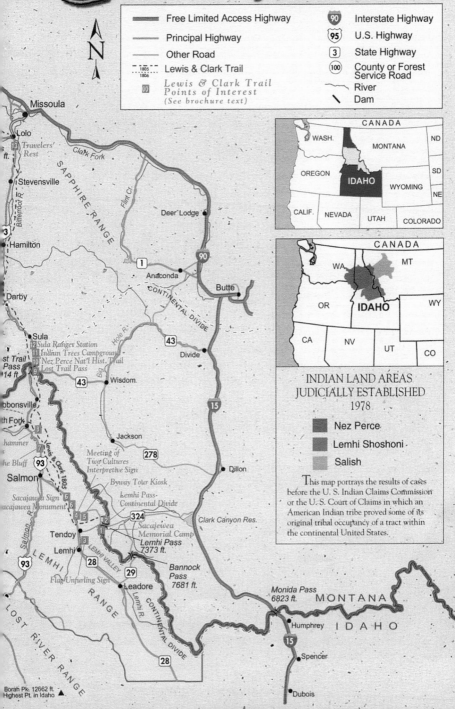

Map Legend:

- Free Limited Access Highway
- Principal Highway
- Other Road
- 1805 / 1806 Lewis & Clark Trail
- 00 Lewis & Clark Trail Points of Interest (See brochure text)
- 90 Interstate Highway
- 95 U.S. Highway
- 3 State Highway
- 100 County or Forest Service Road
- River
- Dam

CANADA
WASH. · MONTANA · ND
OREGON · IDAHO · SD · WYOMING · NE
CALIF. · NEVADA · UTAH · COLORADO

CANADA
WA · MT
OR · IDAHO · WY
CA · NV · UT · CO

INDIAN LAND AREAS JUDICIALLY ESTABLISHED 1978

- Nez Perce
- Lemhi Shoshoni
- Salish

This map portrays the results of cases before the U. S. Indian Claims Commission or the U. S. Court of Claims in which an American Indian tribe proved some of its original tribal occupancy of a tract within the continental United States.

Map locations and labels:

Missoula
Lolo
Travelers' Rest ...ft.
Stevensville
Clark Fork
Flint Cr.
Deer Lodge
Hamilton
SAPPHIRE RANGE
Bitterroot R.
Darby
Anaconda
1
90
Butte
CONTINENTAL DIVIDE
Sula
Sula Ranger Station
Indian Trees Campground
Nez Perce Nat'l Hist. Trail
Lost Trail Pass
st Trail Pass ...14 ft.
43
Wisdom
Divide
43
Hole R.
Big Hole R.
15
bbonsville
th Fork
Jackson
hammer
Lewis & Clark 1805
the Bluff
93
Salmon
Meeting of Two Cultures Interpretive Sign
278
Dillon
Sacajawea Sign
acajawea Monument
Sacajawea R.
Byway Tour Kiosk
Lemhi Pass-Continental Divide
324
Clark Canyon Res.
Sacajewea Memorial Camp
Tendoy
Lemhi Pass 7373 ft.
Lemhi
93
LEMHI RANGE
28
LEMHI VALLEY
29
Leadore
Lemhi R.
Bannock Pass 7681 ft.
Flag Unfurling Sign
Salmon R.
LOST RIVER RANGE
CONTINENTAL DIVIDE
28
Monida Pass 6823 ft.
MONTANA
IDAHO
Humphrey
15
Spencer
Dubois
Borah Pk. 12662 ft. Highest Pt. in Idaho ▲
WYOMING

All parties gathered at Camp Fortunate to prepare for the portage over the mountains.. While preparations were taking place Clark, Sacagawea, Charbonneau and eleven others traveled westward across Lemhi Pass, this time in the company of Chief Cameahwait to his village on the Lemhi River. The oral history of the people describes this event. "We saw her coming with the white men carrying her babe on her back in a wrapped willow cradleboard. She came up over a foothill that had loose shale rocks on one side. They were very careful to walk on the better side of the hill as they came down among us."

After obtaining geographical information from Cameahwait about the Lemhi, Salmon and Bitterroot Rivers as well as the Bitterroot Mountains, Clark left Sacagawea and her husband with the Shoshone and led a reconnaissance party to the Salmon River. They went downstream sixteen and a half miles from the confluence with the North Fork of the Salmon River where it became apparent the river, called "the river of no return" by the Indians, was too dangerous to use for water travel.

After intense trading for twenty-nine horses, the Corps left the Shoshone on their journey overland. They first traveled north across Lost Trail Pass, again crossing the Continental Divide, to the Bitterroot Valley of western Montana where they would meet the Salish. Two Lemhi Shoshone guides, Old Toby and his son, led the way. The Shoshone left to hunt buffalo two days later than they had planned. They had delayed their departure in order to trade and assist the Corps even though they were hungry and in need of meat.

After a dangerous trip over Lost Trail Pass and increasingly bad weather the Corps descended into Ross' Hole, a valley in present-day Montana. There they met the Salish, who were referred to in the journals of Lewis and Clark as the Flathead. A distinct difference between the language of the Shoshone and Salish was described accurately in the journals. Nevertheless, the two Native groups were close and hunted buffalo together. The Salish were generous and kindhearted, evidenced by their willingness to trade healthy horses for the exhausted animals of the Corps. They also sold the group fourteen more horses. Finally, the Corps was ready to head west again, across the divide in search of the Pacific.

Again the Corps parted with their Native friends and began their journey north through the valley to Lolo Creek. On September 9 they camped near the present town of Lolo Mt., at a site they called "Traveler's Rest." Here was the beginning of the formidable Lolo Trail. (They returned the next year and camped in the same place June 30, 1806.) They rested there two days before they set off across what they described as "those terrible mountains." The description is an apt one. They faced the Bitterroot Mountains that border Idaho and Montana, some of the most rugged and inaccessible terrain of the United States, even today. They were forced to kill a horse for food, slept in the snow and were near starvation when they found their way out of the mountains onto the Weippe Prairie of Idaho.

The Lolo Trail

This significant cultural and historical trail across the Bitterroots was the most challenging terrain the Corps encountered. The Lolo Trail was known as the Road to the Buffalo by the Nez Perce and Road to Salmon by the Salish. The Nez Perce hunted buffalo on the plains to the east and the Salish of Montana traveled westward to fish for salmon.

The trail has a life and history of its own. Used for centuries by the Nez Perce and Salish and many other Natives who traveled across these mountains, it initially was a trail for those who walked. When Indians of the region acquired horses around 1700, the trail was modified to connect with meadows to provide horse feed along the way. Rather than remaining close to waterways, those who rode to hunt the buffalo traveled the high country. The Nez Perce name is *Kuseyne 'Iskit*, meaning Buffalo Trail. Some called it the "high water trail," a good trail for hunters. A wagon road was built on part of the trail in 1866 and was called the Bird-Truax Road.

The life-threatening exploration experiences of the Lewis and Clark Expedition do not stand alone in this wilderness. In 1831 John Walk, a Hudson Bay representative from Fort Vancouver, led a party to trade with the Nez Perce. After disappointing results, they began a trek over the Lolo Trail on October 2. Struggling through six feet of snow they found it equally as difficult as had Lewis and Clark. The thirty-five to sixty men, women and children finally reached Packer Meadow on October 13. Their horses had eaten brambles and nearly starved; one died, one gave up and others were

The Dog Seaman

In August, 1803, Lewis set off down the Ohio River from Pittsburgh accompanied by Seaman, his great Newfoundland dog. He had paid $20 for Seaman, a very high price for the time. Floating down the Ohio was easy work to the junction of the Mississippi. He would meet Clark in October in Louisville.

As Seaman set off with Lewis and his party of eleven, he amused himself, as he would constantly on the Voyage of Discovery, by hunting and faithfully presenting his prize to Lewis. On this part of the trip he often jumped overboard to catch swimming squirrels. The Newfoundland breed is a strong swimmer with webbed feet and a love of the water; they are excellent rescue dogs and will pull a drowning person to safety with ease. Seaman had a shining black coat and he had a faithful and brave spirit. He was more than a mascot to the party: his presence interested the Indians along the way and he protected the camp from predators.

The adventures and misadventures of Seaman were noted in the journals. Along the Missouri, while the men sailed and hauled upriver, Seaman loped along the shore, hunting and killing antelope. One day, however, he tried to kill a beaver and was badly wounded with a cut artery in his hind leg. He bled profusely and Lewis thought he might die, but Seaman lived to soon after divert a charging buffalo from the sleeping men.

On the return trip back up the Columbia, Indians at the Cascades stole Seaman. A member of the party had been abducted and Lewis' response was unhesitating. Three men were sent out to recover the dog and ordered to shoot if there was resistance. Seaman was returned.

He was a faithful member of the expedition to the last. When Lewis died on his way to Washington, D.C., after the completion of the expedition, Seaman was taken to live out his days with Clark and to play with the boy Pomp, son of Sacagawea.

lost. The party returned to the Columbia via present-day southern Idaho, choosing not to face the Lolo Trail again.

Tragedy followed the Nez Perce Band of Chief Joseph in 1877 as they fled the troops of General Howard. Chief Joseph had veered away from a journey to bring his people to the reservation when tempers flared and some whites were killed. Fearing retribution, the Nez Perce outmaneuvered the U.S. troops and fled over the Trail, hoping to reach a place of safety in Canada with Sitting Bull. They went in July, with approximately 450 women and children, 250 men and 2,000 horses.

The Trail had been improved in 1866 as a road for wagons by the U.S. government after gold had been discovered at Pierce, Idaho. Lewiston and the surrounding area were booming with commerce and the road was the government's response to merchants who wanted a wagon road to the east. The road was sometimes called the Bird-Truax Road after builders Wellington Bird, engineer, and Major Sewell Truax.

By the time Chief Joseph's band crossed eleven years later, downed timber had clogged the Trail. The Indians left many horses with broken legs and continued on. It was a grueling flight with little food. They crossed the mountains and, after a brutal assault by General Howard's troops, Chief Joseph surrendered with his famous words, "From where the sun now stands, I will fight no more forever." His people were then exiled to Oklahoma Territory where many died.

Roughly, the Lolo Trail parallels Highway 12 and can be traveled today with a permit from the U.S. Forest Service and only from July 1 to October 1. The Clearwater National Forest announces the availability of permits in December for the following year and grants permits through a lottery system. Those selected then have two months to apply for their preferred dates of travel.

The permits will cost $6, with a maximum of ten parties on the trail each day. Each party can have up to ten people and two full-size vehicles, and up to ten horses, bicycles, ATV or motorcycles (as long as the ATVs and motorcycles have noise abatement systems).

Organizations or institutions can also apply for permits to travel the Trail. They can have up to thirty-five people and four vehicles, but only one such large party will be allowed on the Trail each week. Guided hiking, horseback and mountain-bike trips are available.

For more information, you can write or call: Bicentennial Coordinator, Kooskia Ranger Station, Route 1, Box 398, Kooskia, ID 83539; (208) 926-4274. If you completely missed applying, didn't get picked in the lottery or just want to see if you can get in at the last minute you might still have a chance. Unreserved travel dates will be made available on a first-come, first-served basis. Contact www.fs.fed.us/r1/clearwater.

FOLLOWING THE TRAIL
—Scenic Drives and Trail Sites

■ Lewis and Clark Backcountry Byway
[Off Hwy. 28, near Tendoy, ID]
Here is an opportunity to believe, just for a moment, that you were there with Lewis and Clark. When you cross over Lemhi Pass you are crossing the Continental Divide where they did. The high mountain meadows and rolling, jade-colored hills look much the same today as when the expedition journeyed to the top of Lemhi Pass in 1805, where they unfurled the U.S. flag for the first time in the west, beyond the boundaries of the Louisiana Purchase. The party's first campsite in Idaho is marked here. These stands of fir and pine trees are pristine and this thirty-nine-mile trip is rewarding, although it is a graveled road. It is usually closed from November to June and can be muddy in early summer. Allow three hours for the round trip loop from Tendoy.

■ Salmon River Scenic Byway
[From Stanley, ID east on Idaho Hwy. 75 to US 93 at Challis and north to the Montana State line. The length is 162 miles and will take about three and a half hours. This a two-lane road with no passing lanes and some 25 mph curves. Access to the backcountry is best from July to October, although, weather permitting, you might be able to go from April to November.]
The northern end of this byway begins on the Montana border at the Lost Trail Pass (elevation 6,995 feet) where Lewis and Clark struggled down into the Ross' Hole of present-day Montana. The spectacular view from this high point has changed little since then.

The byway follows the course of the Salmon River between Lost Trail Pass and the town of Stanley, ID where three scenic byways meet. The River of No Return, as the Indians referred to the Salmon River, flows through the Salmon-Challis National Forest. The river and its tributaries serve as natural pathways in the rugged Idaho backcountry where deer, elk and moose often graze along the hills and meadows that line this road. You will have a view of the Sawtooth Mountains, other historical sites and wildlife viewing along the route. It is 160 miles long and takes about three and a half hours.

As long as you are at Stanley ID you might want to consider two drives that take three or four hours each, though are not part of the Lewis and Clark Trail. Both of these meet at Stanley.

The Ponderosa Pine Scenic Byway takes you, roughly, from Stanley to Boise ID and provides access to the pristine forests and mountains of Idaho's Sawtooth Wilderness, Salmon-Challis National Forest. This the entryway to the 2.3 million-acre Frank Church River of No Return Wilderness, with more contiguous acres of roadless wilderness than anywhere else in the the lower 48 states.

The Sawtooth Scenic Byway on Idaho Hwy 75 north to Stanley from Shoshone will get you to the world-famous Sun Valley Resort as well as some phenomenal wildlife viewing and geologic attractions at Black Magic Canyon.

The northern end of the Salmon River Scenic Byway begins on the Montana border at the Lost Trail Pass.

■ Lemhi Pass

Lemhi Pass — Continental Divide: milepost 26 of the Back Country Byway, has informal picnicking, rough trailhead and interpretive signs. The expedition crossed this point on August 12, 1805.

Flag Unfurling Sign: milepost 115.8 of Hwy 28 near Tendoy. Tendoy is the entrance to Agency Creek Road, which leads to Lemhi Pass. The dirt road is steep and narrow, generally impassable all winter. Call ahead for information on current conditions, BLM (208) 756-5400. Meriwether Lewis planted the American flag for the first time west of the Rockies and outside the Louisiana Purchase on August 13, 1805.

Meeting of Two Cultures sign: approximately .4 on Alkali Flat Road, which is a milepost 4.1 on Back Country Byway. There are hiking opportunities nearby.

■ Lemhi Valley

Back Country Byway Tour Kiosk: located at milepost 3.7 of the Byway in Idaho. The Byway consists of rough and steep dirt roads that wind through the foothills of the Beaverhead Mountains to Lemhi Pass and back down Agency Creek Road. Carry emergency gear and spare tires. Toilet facilities.

Sacajawea Signs and Monument: milepost 120.5, Hwy 28; famous interpretive sign, milepost 122.5, Hwy 28. Signs celebrate the birthplace of Sacajawea, the Lemhi Shoshone woman who accompanied the expedition. Lewis camped here with the Lemhi Shoshone August 13–14, 1805.

The Bluff has an interpretive sign and campground at milepost 315, US Hwy 93. On August 21, 1805, Clark and party reached the Salmon River and camped near this spot by the bluff near the mouth of Tower Creek. BLM campground.

Wagonhammer Springs at milepost 324, US Hwy 93. Lewis and Clark Trail can be reached by walking 2 miles up West Wagonhammer Creek to Thompson Gulch following the marked trail on the left. Picnic and toilet facilities are available.

Lost Trail Pass, elevation 7,014 feet; Visitors' Center is open during the summer on US Hwy 93 at the Idaho-Montana border. Rest area facilities are available.

■ Bitterroot Valley of Montana

US Hwy 93 and US Hwy 12 intersect at Lolo, MT. These two highways, though not in Idaho, are connected to important trail sites for today's travelers. Places of interest in Montana are listed here.

Traveler's Rest has an interpretive sign near the junction of US Hwys 93 and 12, west of Lolo, Mt. The expedition camped here September 9–11, 1805, and again June 30–July 3, 1806. This site marks the beginning of the Lolo Trail used by the Corps in 1805 and 1806 across the mountains.

Sulu Ranger Station: milepost 11, US Hwy 93S; the ranger station is just south of the "Great Clearing" (Ross's Hole), site of the Salish Village where the expedition spent two nights. Clark camped nearby on his return trip in July, 1806.

Nez Perce National Historic Trail: milepost 7, US Hwy 93S; the trail follows the route taken by the Nez Perce during the war of 1877 and offers an opportunity to hike the area where Clark traveled. An off-highway section is accessed from Hwy 93 south of Indian Trees Campground.

Indian Trees Campground is near milepost 8 on Hwy 93, 2 miles southwest on Forest Road 729. In the Bitterroot Valley and surrounding mountains, scars are often visible on the trunks of century-old Ponderosa pine trees. Salish, Kootenai, Nez Perce and Shoshoni tribes stripped pieces of outer bark to obtain the tree's sweet cambium layer for food. Culturally scarred trees are federally protected.

■ Salmon River Exploration

Milepost 326.1, US Hwy 93. Hoping for an easy trip to the Pacific, William Clark explored the first few miles of the rugged canyon of the Salmon River below here in late August, 1805.

■ The Corps' Trek North

Milepost 345, US Hwy 93. On their way north searching for a route over Idaho's mountain barrier, Lewis and Clark left this canyon and ascended a high ridge to reach the Bitterroot Valley in early September, 1805.

CHAPTER 2

Among the Nez Perce

■ September 22, 1805 ■

On September 22, 1805, the main party of explorers had succeeded in making their way across the most physically grueling and life-threatening section of the entire expedition; they had crossed "the most turrible mountains I ever saw..." according to Sgt. Patrick Gass. They had lost precious weeks in their wanderings between present-day Idaho and Montana looking for the best way over the Continental Divide and had crossed the Divide several times. They met Shoshone and Flathead Indians, encountered a new language, Salish, that sounded like "...a gurgling kind of language spoken much thro the throat," according to Clark. They had traded, given gifts and made promises they could not keep.

They were near starvation. They had lived off the land as they traveled and had many times sustained life on meager portions, at one one point they even killed a wolf and ate it. On September 21 they supped upon three pheasants and duck or two along with the last of the horsemeat. Clark and a party of hunters had gone ahead and returned to meet the main party with a supply of roots, berries and fish obtained from the Nez Perce. Clark's hungry, ragged party, exhausted from the forced march came upon a small party of Nez

Perce digging roots on the Weippe Prairie. The Nez Perce fed them and made them welcome.

"The whites can be our friends, do them no harm," so said Wetxuiis, a Nez Perce woman.

According to the Ni Mii Poo, the Nez Perce's name for themselves, the explorers may not have been as safe as they thought. At first the Ni Mii Poo were alarmed and excited. The explorers looked threatening and strange. Most of the warriors had left earlier to hunt and their defenses were weak.

It seems the explorers, bearded and dirty, didn't know what went on behind the scenes of the camp and would have given little notice to the woman who peered from her tepee when Clark and others appeared. The report of Wetxuiis was not mentioned in the journal writings, but it is an important part of the Nez Perce history.

Except for the determination of Wetxuiis, who had been to the other side of the mountains as a captive, Clark and his small party might have been killed. It was said that she first asked the white man be brought to her, for she was ill, and she spoke to him. Then she ran downstream two miles to Twisted Hair's camp to tell her story.

Oral traditions are taken seriously by people who don't write their histories. The telling and retelling of occurrences result in detail and accuracy that are carried forth for generations. For example, a Nez Perce elder, Totamalweyuon, or Albert Moore as he was later called, told the story of Wetxuiis. He was born in 1861 and clearly remembered the stories told by his people.

Totamalweyuon, or Albert Moore, as he was later called. *Photo: R. R. Beale collection*

"The year before she come through, not Lolo Trail, she came over another trail. She was here at Weippe, where the prairie is. Indians used to camp there, they came from all over to dig camas, from all this reservations and the country, from all over Washington. A lot of people digging camas. And somebody says 'Something's coming! Something strange is coming, some kind of people! It's a man with hair all over his face. Let's go out to get him! They're coming over to the camp, let's get a look at them.'

"Wetxuiis said, 'Don't make a mistake. They are the best kind of people. They are good-hearted people. Friendly people.'

"They all stopped. The chief says, 'Go get them, give them camas and meat.' So they ate camas and meat. That was Lewis and Clark in 1805." So stated Totamalweyuon when he was interviewed around 1960 by Robert Beale.

The Journey of Wetxuiis

Wetxuiis means "Lost from Home then Came Back" and her story of danger and adventure rivals those of the expedition. She was only a small girl, elders say, accompanying her people on a buffalo hunt to the Flathead country of Montana, when she was taken captive by an enemy tribe, possibly the Blackfeet. Her journey was toward the beginning of the day "*tin-na-tit-kinne-kai*" (meaning the east) as she was carried eastward, traded or sold. Ultimately she became the wife of a man, thought to be a Frenchman, that lived somewhere on an island in a big lake. This may have been the Great Lakes area or perhaps the Red River country of Manitoba. A child was born to her there, and when she heard that her husband planned to take her across the Big Water to his homeland, she fled with her baby on her back. White people may have assisted her escape.

It took an entire day to row from the island to the mainland. She carried a hatchet and a small pot for cooking her meals and affirmed her faith in her Wa-yakin, or spirit power, Wolf, to guide her to her homeland, which she knew to be "where the sun sets," or "*tin-ne-nach-et-kinne-kai*."

According to the legend she was indeed guided by Wolf. She began walking westward. When she came to a big river, she simply began making a raft to cross. As she rowed away from shore she saw a grizzly bear coming toward her. In her childhood she had been

Yakima woman and child. Wetxuiis carried her child in a cradleboard much like this one when she made her way home to the Nez Perce.
Moorhous photo, courtesy of Yakima Indian Nation

warned of a long-tailed grizzly that ate people. The spirit power must have given her bravery for she decided to kill the bear and placed her child in the middle of the raft.

With raised war hatchet she waited for the grizzly to approach. When it was near, she gave it one blow to the middle of its huge head. The bear wavered but launched another attack. She struck again. As the bear floated away, bleeding, she caught a glimpse of a long tail.

Wetxuiis continued her journey, walking many days with little food. Soon there was no milk for her child. Her baby died about a day's travel from the Flathead country. She was very close to home for the Flathead were close kin of her people. She buried the child. Sick and grieving, she was found by some Nez Perces who were returning from a hunt and at last was taken over the mountains to her own people.

She spent the rest of her life with her people and was able to serve as a liaison of goodwill for the expedition, perhaps because she recalled earlier kindness by whites. "Lost-from-Home-Then-Came-Back" made the journey before Lewis and Clark and then eased their way with friendship. If she had not spoken out history could have been very different.

The relationship of the Lewis and Clark explorers with the Shahaptian-speaking Nez Perce was pivotal in the success of the expe-

Kate McBeth, missionary to the Nez Perce, shown here with Nez Perce women and children *(back row, second from right)*. McBeth's Indian pupils told her the story of Wetxuiis and the Lewis and Clark Expedition. McBeth's missionary work with the Nez Perce began in 1873. *Photo: National Park Service*

dition and the survival of the explorers themselves. Their driving focus and singularity of purpose never wavered. They had survived the terrible mountains and were now on their way to the Pacific. They knew that Lewis River, the present-day Snake River, was nearby and that it would lead them to the Columbia and the Pacific Ocean. They felt great relief. They were safe and wasted no time in trying to regain their strength. They filled their bellies, became sick from the new diet, hunted, traded and immediately went about gathering information on the best way to proceed to the ocean.

The Snake River upstream from Lyons Ferry and Palouse Falls today. In 1805 it was a wild and free-flowing river with dangerous rapids.

They paid a visit to a nearby chief—Twisted Hair, who had been alerted by Wetxuiis. The chief, camped nearby with his two wives, offered casual hospitality. Outside his shelter he accommodated Lewis by drawing a map on an elk skin and shared meager supplies of food. This was an indicator of the kind of relationship the explorers had with the Nez Perce. They provided friendly assistance without threat or formality.

Camas and Cous
—Bread and Potatoes of the Nez Perce

The prairie where the Nez Perce were camped is an area abundant with camas. This staple of the diet (spelled a multitude of ways in the journals—quamash, quamas, kamsh, kamas, camash, camas, commis, commas, etc.) was also made into a bread called pasheco. Sgt. Gass thought the pasheco tasted a bit like pumpkin bread and called it good and nourishing. This was in spite of the fact that nearly the entire company was stricken with a type of stomach upset due to the change in diet.

Digging for camas was, in fact, what had brought the few Nez Perces to the prairie lands that September. (The present-day Weippe Prairie has been a traditional gathering ground of the Nez Perce for many generations.) As was their annual practice, they had begun root digging in early April and progressed to higher elevations digging onions, camas and cous. An experienced digger could dig roots from a half-acre in a day with a sharp digging stick, a tookas, which was often fitted with an antler handle. Digging roots was women's work and it was believed that the men should not help with the preparation, otherwise it would never get done according to a Nez Perce elder.

The camas bulb is shaped like an onion, yet is sweet. Only the young bulbs of camas were harvested, after the light blue flowers had gone and the seeds had dropped, from July to September. They were cleaned in winnowing trays and the black outer covering removed by hand, leaving a few "whiskers" for flavor. Some of the damaged roots were eaten fresh but the majority were cooked in baking pits for up to three days, meticulously arranged with layers of grass and bulbs over a layer of hot rocks. A fire was then built on top and maintained while the roots steamed below. Most were then

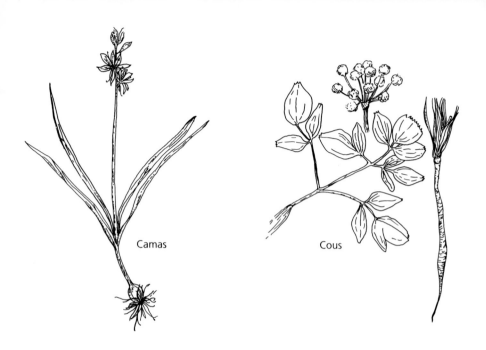

Camas

Cous

dried on racks. The remainder of the steamed roots was shaped into loaves of camas bread or ground in a mortar to be used as meal. Dried camas was stored in caches where it would remain dry and keep indefinitely. The dried bulbs and loaves could then be eaten dry or boiled. Dried camas bulbs require about the same amount of cooking time as dried beans; they swell during cooking, like dried prunes.

Cous was such a source of concentrated food energy that a hunter could be sustained several days with just a small bag of cous. Its cormlike bulb was eaten raw or cooked. Raw, it tastes a bit like parsnip. It was boiled or ground into a meal, then dried and formed into brick-shaped cakes. Because of the resemblance to a stale biscuit, it was commonly called biscuitroot.

When a Nez Perce youth of ten or twelve years was sent on a quest for his guardian spirit, praying and fasting alone, he carried a bag containing five cous roots per day for sustenance.

Serviceberries grow in the canyons along with cous, making the Weippe Prairie a rich source of food. The Nez Perce still gather to dig camas and cous and to collect choke cherries, pine nuts and serviceberries for food as well as medicine plants and fibers for baskets.

FOLLOWING THE TRAIL
—Scenic Drives and Trail Sites

- **Northwest Passage Scenic Byway**

It begins at the junction of US Hwy 12 and US Hwy 95 at Spalding, Idaho, and follows US Hwy 12 northwest to the Idaho-Montana border. It will take about four and a half hours and is 191 miles.

Traveler's Rest just across the border in Montana can be a beginning or an ending point for a trek along the Lewis and Clark Trail in the Pacific Northwest. A section of US Hwy 12 along the Lochsa River in Idaho is designated as the Northwest Passage Scenic Byway. You can experience the vastness of the mountains and forests traversed by the Corps of Discovery. The Byway loosely parallels the Lolo Trail used by the explorers in crossing the Bitterroots.

Along the byway tumbling water is your companion for miles as you make a dramatic passage through the Bitterroots in the Clearwater National Forest. The ridges between the canyons have provided travel corridors for Indians for centuries; wildlife use these same routes to find excellent mountain habitat. These are the trails Lewis and Clark followed. The forest is now well known for its large herds of elk, moose and other big game animals. However, the starving explorers didn't find it so abundant. The animals have taken refuge here in the mountains and forests after civilization encroached on their original lower range and prairie habitat.

Whether you travel east or west you will still be in the footsteps of Lewis and Clark. They traveled essentially the same route both ways—westward in 1805 and on the return trip in 1806. The highway follows the Lochsa River, designated a Wild and Scenic River. This is a pristine area with campgrounds along the river as it flows through the Clearwater National Forest. At Lowell, Idaho, the Selway River joins the Lochsa to form the Middle Fork of the Clearwater River. From the Continental Divide westward the waters are flowing toward the Pacific.

The route is beautiful in any season, but in winter it is possible to encounter snow-covered roads near Lolo Pass at the Montana border. From Kooskia to the Montana border, the highway parallels the largest wilderness area found in the lower forty-eight states; it

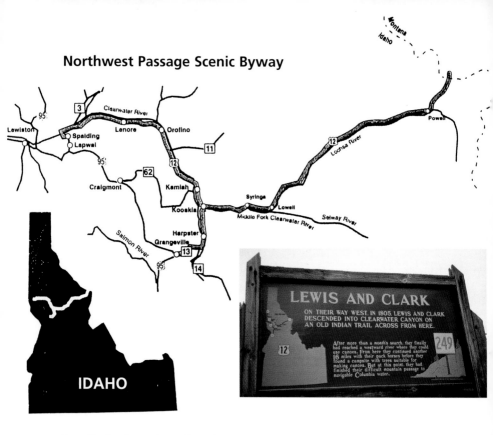

Northwest Passage Scenic Byway

IDAHO

has limited services for about eighty-five miles. There are many places to stop and picnic or camp for the night. Stand by the rushing river, breath deeply and give thanks for something.

Special attractions on the way are Canoe Camp at Orofino, Idaho; Kamiah; Kooskia Crossing Kiosk; Heart of the Monster Park Site; Selway River; Lochsa Historic Ranger Station; Powell Ranger Station; DeVoto Grove; and Lolo Pass Visitor Center.

■ Lolo Hot Springs

On Hwy12, just across the Divide in Montana, this is where Lewis and Clark found the creek dammed by Indians so they could bathe in the warm water. Clark wrote that he found it nearly boiling hot where it came out of the rocks. The expedition camped near this site at Packer Meadow on the return journey June 29, 1806, and bathed in the warm waters. Packer Meadow is almost on the Idaho-Montana border and well marked. There is a commercial hot springs on the highway.

Camping in this wilderness area is available at Kooskia,

Syringa, Lowell and at numerous Forest Service campsites such as Wild Goose, Wilderness Gateway, Jerry Johnson, Wendover, Whitehorse and Whitesands. The byway splits at Kooskia and another loop follows Idaho Hwy 13 from Kooskia to Grangeville and the junction of US 95.

■ Wild and Scenic Rivers

Much of the Northern Region of Idaho and Washington remains remote and wild today. Thanks to the U.S. Congress of 1968, portions of the Lochsa, Selway and Middle Fork of the Clearwater River are components of the National Wild and Scenic Rivers System.

...certain rivers of the Nation which, with their immediate environments, possess outstandingly remarkable scenic, recreational, geologic, fish and wildlife, historic, cultural, or other similar values, shall be preserved in free-flowing condition, and that they and their immediate environments shall be protected for the benefit and enjoyment of present and future generations...
— WILD AND SCENIC RIVERS ACT, October 2, 1968

■ Lolo Trail Motorway

Milepost 174.4, US Hwy 12. For the very adventurous and well equipped, the Lolo Trail Motorway closely follows this the Lolo Trail of the Nez Perce used by the explorers. This route is a rugged mountain pass, not a highway, so be prepared. It generally parallels US Hwy 12 from Lolo, Montana, to a few miles west of Lolo Pass. Then it follows the high mountain ridges north of the highway for more than eighty miles, eventually descending to the Weippe Prairie near Weippe, Idaho. Before you consider taking this trip be sure to consult the Clearwater National Forest folks at Orofino or Powell Ranger Station; you must have a permit to go through here. The Lolo Trail Motorway is a primitive dirt road and most sections are not designed to accommodate low-clearance vehicles, trailers or large recreational vehicles. Those who take the two-day trip from Powell to Weippe will find a few rustic campsites with minimum facilities along the way. Adequate supplies of fuel, fresh water, food and warm clothing should be carried.

The Lewis and Clark party crossed over the Lolo Trail Crossing on September 13, 1805, westbound for the ocean. They struggled in

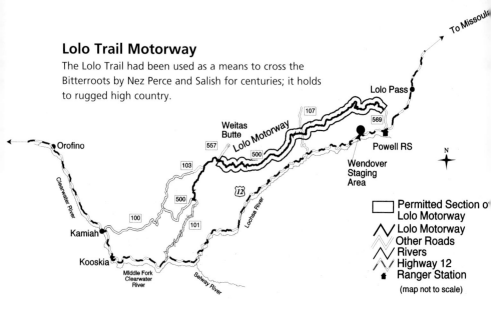

Lolo Trail Motorway

The Lolo Trail had been used as a means to cross the Bitterroots by Nez Perce and Salish for centuries; it holds to rugged high country.

deep snow across Lolo Trail, which followed steep ridges for 125 miles to the Clearwater River.

Lolo Pass Visitor and Information Center is on the Idaho-Montana border at an elevation of 5,235 feet. Ancient Indian travel routes from north, south, east and west intersect at this point, the most significant of which is the east/west Lolo Trail. The Clearwater National Forest operates a visitor information center here during the summer months.

▪ Weippe, Idaho

Milepost 17.2, Hwy 11. Off the beaten path from US Hwy 12, take the highway between Ofoino and Kamiah cross the Clearwater River at Greer and follow the signs upriver to Weippe. This is an out of the way place in Idaho where you can actually see the prairie where Lewis and Clark first encountered the Nez Perce. Travel with caution and get local information before you drive it in the winter. The steep grade from river level to the prairie above is full of switchbacks. When the sign says 15 mph believe it and watch for logging trucks. The view from turnouts is spectacular and gives you a chance to get a sense of the terrain.

After meeting the Nez Perce on the Weippe Prairie the explorers came down the steep trail to the narrow, rushing Clearwater River. Even though the site of meeting the Nez Perce is presently a

Weippe Prairie near Weippe ID, where Lewis and Clark first encountered the Nez Perce at the camas digging grounds. This is now a pasture and there is an informative sign at the site.

pasture for cattle you can find it along a gravel road just outside of Weippe. Follow the sign on the right just as you enter town. During the summer months the blue flowers of camas still bloom here.

■ Food for the Corps

Milepost 252.9, US Hwy 12. On May 31, 1806, Sgt. John Ordway and Pvts. Frazer and Wiser began the return trip from Lewis River (Snake River) with salmon for the Corps of Discovery who waited at Camp Choppunish (Kamiah). After crossing the Camas Prairie near here the group arrived two days later with seventeen salmon and some roots they had purchased. Although most of the fish were spoiled, Lewis described those that were sound as "extremely delicious."

■ Trading for Food

Milepost 268.6, US Hwy 95. On May 27, 1806, Sgt. John Ordway and Pvts. Frazer and Weiser were dispatched from Camp Choppunish (Kamiah) to Lewis River (Snake River) to obtain salmon. With Nez Perce guides they crossed the Camas Prairie near here. At the Salmon River, Frazer traded an old razor for two Spanish mill dollars and the party proceeded to the Snake River over tortuous terrain where they purchased a number of salmon.

■ Nez Perce Village

Milepost 306.8, US Hwy 95. This important archeological site was occupied for 10,000 years or more and has at least ten pit houses that are as much as 5,000 years old. This village reached its height from about 4,100 to 2,600 years ago but remained important enough that when fur traders arrived in 1812 they made this their main camp.

■ Canoe Camp

US Hwy 12. This is the site of Lewis and Clark's dugout canoe building activity for two weeks. On Hwy 12 near Orofino, Idaho, this camp is on the Clearwater River across from the confluence of the North Fork, where Dworshak Dam is located. At Canoe Camp the group recuperated from their forced march over the mountains and set about making canoes. After failed attempts they enlisted the expertise of building dugout canoes from the Nez Perce who efficiently burned the centers of the logs. It took ten days to build five canoes. They next branded their horses and left them in the care of Nez Perce Chief Twisted Hair. From this site, October 7, 1805, they launched their westward journey by water to the Pacific.

There is an interpretive walk and picnic site at this location. You can still see the beauty and crystal clear water of the river described by Sgt. Gass in his journal. The stony river bottom and banks are composed of colorful round stones and looking into the bottom of this river is a delightful experience. Although it is not completely free flowing and there are fewer salmon now, it is still an intriguing waterway all the way upriver from Lewiston, Idaho, where you leave the backwaters of the small Washington Water Power Dam.

■ Potlatch Creek Rapids

This is the site of a canoe mishap October 8, 1805. Off US Hwy 12, about eight miles upriver from Lewiston, drive to the north end of Arrow Bridge and turn onto Hwy 3. Three-tenths of a mile northeast, their camp lay on the small flat along the west side of the creek, close on the right side of the road. Sgt. Patrick Gass wrote, "In the evening, in passing through a rapid, I had my canoe stove, and she sunk. Fortunately the water was not more than waste deep, so our lives and baggage were saved, though the latter was wet." They camped nearby to repair the damage and dry out. They also camped on the downriver side of Potlatch Creek on their return trip.

■ Nez Perce National Historic Park Headquarters

Spalding, Idaho, US Hwy 95. You can visit the museum and interpretive center there and get an overview of the other sites. As you drive watch for the road markers with two crossed feathers that mark other sites within the park.

- **Chief Timothy State Park & Alpowai Interpretive Center**
West of Clarkston, Washington, on US Hwy 12, this site has an audiovisual presentation and exhibits on Indian history and culture and the Lewis and Clark Expedition. This park is on the an island created by the backwaters of Lower Granite Dam, which was the site of a large camp of Shahaptian-speaking Indians at the mouth of Alpowai Creek, noted in the journals.

- **Palouse Falls State Park**
Off US Hwy 261. Located six miles north of adjacent to Lyons Ferry State Park near the confluence of the Snake River and Palouse (Drewer's) River, which the Corps passed in their rapid descent to the sea, an average of fifty-eight miles per day. There is an easy short trail from parking lot to an overlook of a 190-foot waterfall. Look for wildlife.

- **Wolf Education and Research Center (WERC)**
Winchester, Idaho, US Hwy 95. Located on the outskirts of town, take a self-guided tour and learn the ways of the gray wolf with the resident ten-member pack. There are displays and exhibits at the longhouse visitor center. Winchester State Park is nearby with camping and yurts for sleeping. The 104-acre forested lake has great fishing and more chances to view wildlife.

- **Heart of the Monster Nez Perce National Historical Park**
East Kamiah, Idaho, US Hwy 12. In Nez Perce legend Coyote the Trickster heard of a monster that was devouring all the inhabitants of the Kamiah Valley. He armed himself with five sharp stone knives and a fire drill and came to the valley to destroy the monster. Coyote tricked the monster into inhaling him. Inside the monster, Coyote lit the fat surrounding the monster's heart on fire, which allowed the animals eaten by the monster to escape in the smoke through openings in the monster's body. Coyote severed the monster's head and escaped. Once he was free, Coyote cut pieces from the dead monster's body and cast them to locations near and far through the known world to create all other Indian tribes. Coyote then created the noble Ni Mii Poo (Nez Perce) from the enormous heart's blood to inhabit the Kamiah Valley and surrounding mountains, plateaus and valleys. Gradually the monster's heart turned to

stone and to this day remains visible protruding from the earth in the center of the Heart of the Monster Nez Perce National Historical Park.

■ Hell's Canyon

Access via boat travel is at Lewiston, Idaho, and Clarkston, Washington. This is the deepest gorge in North America, half again deeper than the Grand Canyon. The Snake River in Hell's Canyon is one of the few whitewater rivers available to powerboats. Several outfitters and guides offer float trips through the canyon for whitewater excitement or you can take a tour boat upriver. Hell's Gate State Park at Lewiston offers camping and picnicking by the river. The Hell's Canyon National Recreation Area includes Hell's Canyon Wilderness and the sixty-seven miles of Wild and Scenic Snake River. Information centers are in Riggins Idaho, Clarkston, Washington, and Enterprise, Oregon.

■ Dworshak Fisheries Complex

Ahsakha, Idaho, US Hwy 12. The complex offers free tours. Steelhead trout and chinook salmon young are raised here.

■ Lower Monumental Lock and Dam

Kahlotus, Washington, US Hwy 12. The dam provides a viewing room and fish displays.

OPPOSITE PAGE

Above: Palouse Falls, Palouse Falls State Park, WA. This is a good place to see an example of the basaltic flows which covered the Columbia River Basin eons ago.

Below: The last of the Palouse. This small Shahaptian-speaking tribe lived in the area where the Palouse River empties into the Snake in Washington. They steadfastly refused to move onto a reservation and quietly disappeared into poverty and memory over the years. These photographs were taken in 1913–14.
Photo: R. R. Beale Collection

CHAPTER 3

Introduction to the Big River

■ October 16, 1805 ■

The Lewis and Clark Expedition reached the Columbia River near present-day Pasco, Washington, on October 16, 1805. They had traveled, according to their estimate, 3714 miles, over seventeen months. They saw the Big River with a keen sense of accomplishment because they knew it would take them to the Pacific Ocean. The Columbia is indeed big and rolling, and in 1805, before the advent of dams, its power was undiminished. In flood season it raged. Fortunately, the explorers made their down-river trip on the Snake and Columbia in the season of lower water. While they were able to manage the dangerous rapids in the fall, it would have been disastrous to attempt it during spring runoff.

They had barely made their camp at the confluence of the Snake and Columbia at the site of present-day Sacajawea Park when they were greeted with a drumming and singing entourage led by a chief from a camp about a quarter mile upriver. These were Wanapums and Yakimas, linguistically related to the Nez Perce so their guides could easily translate. The captains gave medals, handkerchiefs and a shirt to the chiefs; the pair purchased seven dogs and were given fish and about twenty pounds of very fat dried horsemeat. This was their first

PEACE MEDAL (front and back).
Lewis and Clark left peace medals like this along the route, usually with chiefs. Prized possessions, they were buried with the owner at times. One unearthed near the confluence of the Potlatch and Clearwater Rivers in Idaho in 1899 during railroad construction was probably the medal that Clark had given to Chief Twisted Hair.

Another was found in 1968 at the burial site of a young Palouse man at the mouth of the Palouse River. The owner of the medal was buried in a canoe coffin. A report in 1854 described a Palouse chief, Wattai-Wattai-How-Lis, who proudly exhibited such a medal and stated it had been given to his father, Ke-Pow-Han.
Photo: National Park Service

look at a vast salmon fishing culture of the Columbia. There were salmon everywhere, dead, dying, drying and being caught.

At the fishing villages they visited on the Columbia near Pasco, Clark was invited into one of the lodges and furnished a mat to sit on. He described the experience in his journal. Clark was a creative speller and sometimes took liberties with variations of spelling the same word. This is just fine with us, we only wish we had been there.

RECIPE FOR SALMON (by William Clark)

...and one man set about preparing me something to eate, first he brought in a piece of Drift log of pine and with a wedge of the elks horn, and a malet of stone curiously carved he Split the log into Small pieces and lay'd it open on the fire on whch he put round Stones, a woman handed him a basket of water and a large Salmon about half driedd, when the Stones were hot he put them into the basket of water with the fish which was soon sufficiently boiled for use it was then taken out put on a platter of rushes neatly made, and set before me ... after eateing the boiled fish which was delicious, I set out.

45

The Route of Lewis & Clark in Washington State

Long Beach
Illwaco
Naselle
7/15-24
11/10-14
11/8
S.R. 4
11/6
Longview
Interstate 5
Oregon
Pacific Ocean
3/29
11/4
3/30
3/31-4/1-6
Vancouver
Bonneville Dam
Columbia River
11/1
4/10-11
10/30-31
4/12
4/13
10/29
4/14
4/18
10/24
10/22-23
4/19-20
10/21
The Dalles Dam
4/21
John Day Dam

By the time they left that camp two days later they had purchased another forty dogs, by now the preferred meat of most of
the men. On October 18, 1805, the explorers continued downriver
by water. Just downstream from the mouth of the Walla Walla
River the Columbia swings hard to the west and enters a series of
deep gorges between this point and the eastern slopes of the Cascades. The journal entries note the significant change in the terrain
here. They were now entering Wallula Gap, a picturesque landmark that marks the beginning of a narrowing gorge, which was
formed by repeated and cataclysmic floods at the end of the ice
age, 12,000 to 15,000 years ago.

Wallula Gap on the Columbia River.

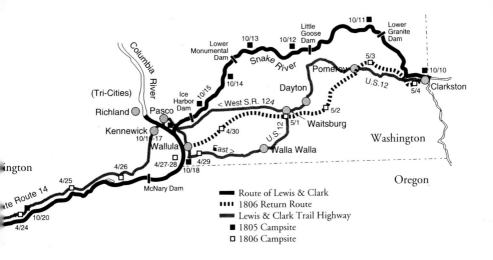

That night they camped just below the Walla Walla River confluence near Two Sisters and were visited by some Walla Wallas and their chief, Yellept, who befriended them. Later he would help them on the return journey. Lewis took a vocabulary and determined they were linguistically related to the Nez Perce. The two Nez Perce chiefs who served as interpreters for the Lewis and Clark party, Twisted Hair and Tetoharksy (Big Horn), were helpful in establishing friendly relations and in finding a safe passage through rapids.

From a high point Clark spotted Mt. Hood. The explorers were not aware they were seeing Mt. Hood and called it Timm or Falls Mountain for a time. The captains had information from Captain George Vancouver's expedition thirteen years earlier to the North Pacific. Vancouver had sighted Mt. Hood, elevation 11,225 ft, from the coast. Lewis had taken tracings from Vancouver's Voyages that included this topographical information on a large inclusive map that was used during the expedition. This working map was not complete, but it did locate Mt. Hood, Mt. St. Helens and Mt. Rainier.

Further downstream, near the mouth of the Umatilla River, Clark sighted what he thought to be Mt. St. Helens, however, it is likely he saw Mt. Adams, since Mt. St. Helens would not be visible from where he was.

Below present-day Hat Rock, Oregon, were the Umatilla Rapids, which Clark named the Musselshell for the heaps of shell middens found there and all along the Columbia. These shells were from the freshwater mussels, an important food item for the Indians. Here Clark shot a sandhill crane and found that he had so frightened peo-

Drying fish on the Umatilla River. Salmon were still abundant at the turn of the century on tributaries of the Columbia and Indians continued to dry them in the traditional way. *Moorhous photo, courtesy of Yakima Indian Nation*

ple in a village on the opposite shore (in present-day Washington), that they had shut themselves in their lodges. Clark wrote they would not be comforted until the chiefs, the Nez Perce guides, arrive to interpret. It seems they had never seen a gun before and when they saw the crane fall from the sky in a clap of thunder they said "we came from the clouds, etc. and were not men, etc." All ended well when Clark gave gifts and the chiefs explained the situation.

Mt St. Helens

This is the same Mt. St. Helens that erupted violently and suddenly May 18, 1980. An earthquake of 5.1 magnitude triggered a slide on the bulging north slope and was immediately followed by an intense explosion of superheated gases, which spewed out 3 to 4 billion yards of rock debris, glacial ice and ash that traveled 70 to 150 mph. The slide buried the valley of the North Fork of the Toutle River with 50–600 feet of debris and layered 0.6 cubic mile of debris over twenty-five square miles. Unexpectedly the side literally blew off the mountain. This lateral blast of gases, rocks, steam and ash quickly overtook the avalanche and accelerated up to the speed of sound. All life for up to twenty-three miles away was wiped out and 150,000 acres of forest nineteen miles away were crushed.

Those who watched in the northwest saw a vertical plume with

Horse Heaven Hills, Columbia River. Sgt. Patrick Gass wrote in his journals about the abundance of horses on these hills. They were not wild horses, but belonged to the nearby Yakimas.

a purple, cauliflower-shaped cloud edged with lightning that spewed out 540 million tons of ash and pumice at least 12 miles into the air over a period of nine hours. The ash drifted down on 22,000 square miles over the northwest and circled the earth during the next two weeks.

A vast, gray landscape lay where once the forested slopes of Mt. St. Helens grew. In 1982, President Reagan and Congress created the 110,000-acre National Volcanic Monument for research, recreation and education. Inside the monument, the environment is left to respond naturally to the disturbance. Yet, life returned in a surprisingly short period of time. Trees began to sprout on slopes, trout and steelhead returned to the streams, and approximately 600 elk had returned within four years.

FOLLOWING THE TRAIL
—Scenic Drives and Trail Sites

■ Sacajawea State Park
Pasco, Washington, US Hwy 12. The expedition spent October 16 and 17, 1805, at the site of Sacajawea State Park at the confluence of the Snake and Columbia Rivers. The park is one mile off Hwy 12 near Pasco, Washington. Leaving Pasco downriver, just before the

bridge across the Snake, turn right. Exhibits here highlight the role of Sacajawea in the success of the expedition. Here, her name is spelled in the old way; today the usual spelling is Sacagawea. This is a shaded park that provides an opportunity to quietly watch the flow of the Columbia and consider the Horse Heaven Hills across the river and how they have changed little since Lewis and Clark were there. The half-wild herds of horses between The Dalles and the Snake River especially impressed Sgt. Patrick Gass, who declared he had seen "more horses, than I ever before saw in the same space of country." Geese and hawks abound; a museum and fishing are on the site.

■ Hat Rock State Park
9 miles east of Umatilla, Oregon, US Hwy 730. On October 19, 1805, Clark climbed this basalt formation and saw what he thought was Mt. St. Helens but was most likely Mt. Adams. It is possible to hike to Hat Rock from the park that has interpretive signs, hiking and fishing.

■ McNary Dam Overlook
East of Umatilla, Oregon, US Hwy 730. Interpretive signs describe the Umatilla Rapids seen from this dam. The Corps met Umatilla villagers northwest of here.

■ Irrigon Marine Park
West of Umatilla, Oregon, US Hwy 730. The Corps camped near the park shore here. Firewood was scarce and "...about 100 Indians came and a number of them brought wood, which they gave us," William Clark, October 19, 1805. The park has interpretive signs.

■ Crow Butte State Park
West of Patterson, Washington, State Route 14. The island park is accessible by a causeway in the pool behind John Day Dam. It is on the route traversed by the Expedition.

■ LePage Park
East of Biggs, Oregon, I-84. The park is near John Day River and John Day Dam. The park was named for the Corp's Pvt. Jean LePage by Lewis and Clark. There are interpretive signs.

■ McNary National Wildlife Refuge and McNary Environmental Education Center

Hwy 12. Access the Education Center a quarter mile off Hwy 12 downriver from the Snake River Bridge near Burbank, Washington. This refuge spans the east bank of the Columbia from the Snake River to the Wallula Gap. It features hiking trails, wildlife viewing and the education center. There is a mile-long hiking trail through area with hawks eagles and falcons; there is also fishing. The refuge is open daily from dawn to dusk.

The wildlife viewing blind at the education center is a treasure. Be prepared to see quail, magpies, turtles, frogs, fish, muskrats, ducks, geese and to identify specific birds like marsh wrens, yellow-headed blackbirds and red-winged blackbirds. If you have been driving and need respite this is it, better than another coffee and barely off the highway. This is the kind of place that helps us remember that this is our planet to care for. Take sketchbooks and cameras.

■ Tmastslikt Cultural Institute

I-84. This interpretive center is on the Umatilla Indian Reservation, take exit 216 off the highway. There are Lewis and Clark exhibits and interpretative exhibits of the Indians who greeted the Corps of Discovery in the Columbia Plateau region.

■ Wallula Wayside, Two Sisters

Pasco, WA Hwy 73. This site is a roadside interpretation of the "Two Sisters" legend from the local tribes and a trail to that rock formation. It is a natural monument comprised of basalt pillars from the volcanic flows over the region 15,000 years ago. Overlooking the Columbia River, two miles southwest of Pasco on WA 73. The legend is that Coyote the Trickster, turned two beautiful sisters into stone in a rage of jealousy.

■ Umatilla National Wildlife Refuge

Irrigon, Oregon, US Hwy 730. McCormack Unit of the refuge offers a spectacular look at a variety of wildlife, from deer lounging in the tall grasses to a multitude of waterfowl and migrating birds. To reach McCormack Unit take Patterson Ferry Road toward the river off US Hwy 730 five miles west of Umatilla.

The refuge is a mix of open water, slough, shallow marsh, ripar-

Umatilla National Wildlife Refuge.

ian woodlands, seasonal wetlands, crop land, islands and shrub-steppe upland habitats. It is divided into six units, two in Oregon, three in Washington and one unit midriver. The scarcity of wetlands and other natural habitats in this area make Umatilla Refuge vital to migrating waterfowl, bald eagles, nesting birds and other migratory and resident wildlife.

This is a highly recommended stop. Plan to take time to go slowly and breathe in nature. You might notice a pair of eyes watching you and then disappear as a doe and fawn glide away.

■ Mt. St. Helens National Volcanic Monument Visitor Center

Amboy, Washington, State Hwy 504. The center reveals tremendous views of Mt. St. Helens, including the crater, lava dome and blast zone. Mt. St. Helens Visitor Center, Coldwater Ridge Visitor Center, and Johnston Ridge Observatory are open daily during the summer months. Interpretive talks, walks and theater programs are offered at each site.

■ Lewis and Clark Confluence Project

Look for sculptures by the famed architect/artist Maya Lin created for the Washington Lewis and Clark Bicentennial. They will be installed at the major confluences that provided Lewis and Clark their passage to the "End of Voyage": Clearwater/Snake, Snake/Columbia, Willamette/Columbia and the Columbia at the Pacific.

CHAPTER 4

The Falls and Chinookan Traders

▪ October 22, 1805 ▪

...Here we landed a few minits to Smoke...6 miles below the upper mouth of Towornehiooks (Deschutes) River the commencement of the pitch of the great falls... we landed and walked down accompanied by an old man to view the falls (Celilo), and the best rout for to make a portage...

— CLARK journal entry

The journals were punctuated with descriptions of rapids. Many were termed "bad rapids" and "verry bad rapids" as they approached the narrows of the Columbia. They saw numerous Indians who observed them as they passed and they stopped often to smoke and talk.

Clark calculated the downriver trip from the Snake River to Celilo Falls was 151 miles and that same distance on to the ocean. They reached Celilo Falls, which they termed The Great Falls of the Columbia, in five days

The Corps of Discovery had hoped for a float trip from the divide to the ocean. It was not to be, and the roughest of all the waters they encountered was the fifty-five miles of rapids and churning waters in narrow passages that began with Celilo Falls, thirty-eight feet high. They portaged their supplies around Celilo

Falls on the north side, then took the dugouts to the other side where they were dragged around the falls close below the present-day boat landing at Celilo Park. Camp that nightwas across the river on a sandbar on the Washington side. Just below Celilo falls the explorers began to see large numbers of seal that they thought were sea otters.

The Columbia River Gorge is a spectacular river canyon with eighty miles of gorgeous scenery, up to 4,000 feet deep in places as it cuts the only sea-level route through the Cascade Mountain Range. In November, 1986, Congress recognized the unique beauty of the Gorge and designated it the nation's first National Scenic Area.

The geography of the Columbia Gorge is dramatic, particularly at The Dalles. Here, where the river narrows, the Indians created fishing stations where fish could be easily speared as they migrated past, crowded together in great numbers from one side of the river to the other. The warm winds that blow up the gorge created an ideal place for fishing and trading villages 200 years ago; now they make this a playground for the windsurfers of the world.

The main village of the Wishram Indians was on the north bank near present-day Wishram, WA. It was called Nixluidix, meaning "Trading Place" and it was here that the most intense trading took place. Across the river the Wasco Indians occupied the present-day Oregon side.

The Dalles, at the present day city of The Dalles, Oregon, consisted of a quarter mile of Short Narrows that Clark described as "agitated gut Swelling, boiling & whorling in every direction." They actually shot these rapids with the canoes "...to the astonishment of all the Indians ... who viewed us from the top of the rock" (Clark).

The Dalles was a significant dividing line between Northwest Coast and Plateau Indians and between the two great linguistic families—Shahaptian and Chinookan. The Shahaptian chiefs who had accompanied the expedition from the Clearwater, Tetoharsky and Twisted Hair, were ready to leave. They stated, correctly, that they could no longer interpret. They were persuaded to stay a couple more days while the explorers effected what they thought was a peace treaty between the Shahaptians and the Chinookans. Gifts and medals were given followed by dancing and fiddle playing in the evening. However, the claim that they had negotiated a treaty was an illusion. The explorers had little understanding of the complexities of intertribal politics and to claim they had negotiated a treaty was presumptuous. The next day Tetoharsky and Twisted Hair took their leave to return upriver. They would again meet the explorers on their return trip.

After the stomach-churning Short Narrows came the Long Narrows, which were as dangerous. Men who could not swim and valuable articles were sent around the Long Narrows and the canoes were sent through, two at a time, steered by the experienced boatmen. After this day-long torture they gave themselves a chance to rest for three days at "Fort Rock." They used this same camp on the return trip. The churning trip took nine days from Celilo Falls to this point at the present-day The Dalles, Oregon.

The canoes they used were the dugouts made of Ponderosa pines constructed a month earlier in present-day Idaho. Dugouts worked well for the Nez Perce, who instructed in making them, but they were bulky and hard to manage in white water.

Continuing on, they passed the Klickitat, Hood and White Salmon Rivers. The Columbia creates a great gash through the Cascade Mountains here, and the water flowing to the river creates beautiful waterfalls. The most spectacular falls can be seen on the Oregon side of the river.

Forty-five miles below The Dalles came the final obstacle—the Cascades, or Grand Rapids, of the Columbia. This time they faced four miles of continuous falls and chutes. It took two days to descend that four-mile stretch. They walked around the obstacles single-file, Sacagawea carrying her baby. The empty canoes were floated through.

Dams in the Columbia Gorge

As we stand at the sites along this area today, we can only see the slow-moving waters created by John Day, The Dalles and Bonneville Dams. These dams impounded more than the picturesque falls and frightening rapids that Lewis and Clark found there. The narrows of the Columbia Gorge and its rich fishing grounds had been the home and livelihood to thousands of Indians for centuries. The total number of salmon and ocean-going trout is thought to be

Fishing at Celilo Falls before the backwaters of John Day Dam covered the falls. Indians fished here for thousands of years, taking advantage of an incredible number of migrating salmon. In historic times the estimates are 123 million pounds were harvested each year. Salmon was the main staple along with a large variety of other fish. *Photo: R. R. Beale collection*

Journal Entry, October 22, 1805 by William Clark

"I observe great numbers of Stacks of pounded Salmon neatly preserved in the following manner, i.e., after [being] suffi[ci]ently Dried it is pounded between two Stones fine, and put into a speces of basket neatly made of grass and rushes better than two feet long and one foot Diamiter, which basket is lined with Skin of Salmon Stretched and dried for the purpose in this it is pressed down as hard as is possible when full they Secure the open part with fish Skins across which they fasten thro. The loops of the basket that part very securely, and then on a Dry Situation they Set those baskets the corded part up, their common custome is to Set 7 as close as they can Stand and 5 on top of them, and secure them with mats which is raped around them and made fast with cords and covered with mats, those 12 baskets of from 90 to 100 lbs. Each for a Stack. Thus preserved those fish may be kept Sound and sweet Several years, as those people inform me, Great quantities as they inform us are sold to the white people who visit the mouth of this river as well as to the natives below."

between 10 and 15 million a year at the time. Thanks to dams, since then the population has been decimated and some species no longer exist.

These fishing grounds supported a dense population of Indians strung out along the riverbanks, or concentrated in trading centers from Celilo Falls downstream past The Dalles. It was a place of trade and cultural exchange and various languages could be heard here as Yakimas, Wanapums, Wallulas, Umatillas, Wishrams, Teninos, Watlalas, Multnomahs, Kathlamets and Wahkiakums came to exchange goods. At Nixluidix, the Corps saw towering stacks of salmon, which Clark estimated to be about 10,000 pounds each. There were three major salmon runs from spring through fall, but it was the fall season that brought the biggest runs, and that is when fishing and trading intensified.

Great Markets of Trade on the Columbia —The Pacific-Plateau Trade System

As the explorers continued down the Columbia they found the Indians traded warily and showed signs of distrust. They also saw increasing evidence of trade with Europeans. By the time they reached the John Day River, non-Native clothing and implements were abundant. All of this was a precursor to strained and often tense relations between river Indians and expedition members. They had encountered a sophisticated and far-ranging market and trade structure—the Pacific Plateau System. At the narrowest gorge of the lower Columbia River the salmon crowded together in their migrations upstream and the Indians plucked them out by the tons. The Chinookan-speaking traders of the area were middlemen to a trade network that stretched from the Pacific Coast to the mountains of present-day Idaho.

Yakimas, Teninos, Umatillas, Wallulas and Nez Perce came downriver to trade and socialize. Those nearby brought meat, roots and berries to exchange for fish and European cloth and ironware. Nez Perce who had access to the plains brought skin clothing, horses and buffalo meat. They were mostly interested in beads, metal and European goods.

The coastal Chinookans came upriver to trade in efficient, elegant canoes laden with coastal fish, roots, berries and wappato roots that would be pounded and made into bread. European manufactured goods obtained from fur traders and ships that occasionally visited the coast were in great demand upriver. They brought with them guns, blankets, clothing, trinkets and the sought-after blue beads. At The Dalles these items were traded for dried salmon, buffalo meat and bear grass used in making cooking baskets and fine Northwest Coast hats.

Without a doubt a trading trip was also a chance to meet friends, strengthen alliances and family ties and to vie for attention from the opposite sex. It was estimated later that as many as 3,000 Indians traded at the Wishram villages at the peak of the season.

The Chinookans who maintained control of the trade center were in fact maintaining a balance of power that was reflected in attitudes toward the Lewis and Clark expedition. They found the Indians along the stretch between Celilo Falls and the Cascades to be more antagonistic and troublesome than those encountered before. Stealing was a growing problem and on the return journey Lewis actually threatened to fire on thieves.

While the explorers felt the Indians were untrustworthy they were missing a more subtle aspect of a complex issue. The traders of the Columbia had long held control and expected tribute from others that came to trade. While the members of the expedition gave token gifts and traded, the Indians had helped them to avoid disaster in the rapids. It seems that pilfering a few items from the explorers was a way to remind that respect must be paid to the powerful middlemen of the Pacific Plateau System. Surely they were not a thieving culture; stacks of valuable fish were left in their villages with no thought of theft.

Considering the language and cultural barriers, it is not surprising that there would be this kind of misunderstanding.

FOLLOWING THE TRAIL
—Scenic Drives and Trail Sites

■ The Columbia River Gorge National Scenic Area
This is the only sea-level passage through the Cascade Mountain Range—the passage the Lewis and Clark expedition sought and found.

By definition, a National Scenic Area is designated to protect rural and scenic resources while community growth and development are encouraged. Unique natural features of the Columbia River Gorge combine with being an important transportation corridor for the northwest.

The Gorge has supported flourishing civilizations for more than 31,000 years. Evidence of the Folsom and Marmes people, who crossed from Asia, has been found in archaeological digs. Excavations at Five Mile Rapids, a few miles east of The Dalles, show humans have occupied this ideal salmon-fishing site for more than 10,000 years.

The Gorge presents plenty of opportunities to identify varying geologic formations. The geologic story of the Gorge began 40 million years ago with the fiery volcanoes of the Cascade Range. Over the centuries, these volcanoes left lava and mudflows up to two miles thick, and you can still see remnants of these flows in the Gorge cliffs. The Columbia River actually cut a deep canyon through all those layers of lava, ash and mud.

Near the end of the last ice age, about 15,000 year ago, cataclysmic floods up th 1,200 feet deep swept down the river corridor. Cliffs were scoured and the tributary streams were left hanging high above the river's bed. As a result, we now have one of the world's greatest concentrations of waterfalls in all their beauty. Massive landslides further altered the walls of the Gorge; in fact, a recent slide can be seen off I-84 at Dodson, where a wide flow of debris moved houses and wiped out a community's infrastructure in 1966.

It is easy to navigate through the Columbia River Gorge. State Hwy 14 on the Washington side and Interstate 84 on the Oregon side are the main highways along the river. Four bridges help you from one side of the river to the other: Cascade Locks/Stevenson; Hood River/Bingen; The Dalles/Dallseport; and Biggs/Maryhill. Buckle up, drive safely and enjoy!

On State Hwy 14 on the Washington side of the Columbia River Gorge you will find views of Mt. Adams and Mt. St. Helens and a chance to stop at Bingen or White Salmon to sample local wines or fruits. At Wind River relax at Carson Hot Mineral Springs Resort.

On the Oregon side, one of two drivable stretches of the Historic Columbia River Highway is between Mosier at Exit 69 and

The Dalles. This series of loops takes you to the top of Rowena Plateau and the Governor Tom McCall Preserve, a wildflower refuge maintained by the Nature Conservancy.

The Historic Columbia River Highway is comprised of two segments and runs roughly parallel to the river and Interstate 84. It will return you to I-84 where you can choose one of several bridges to cross to the Washington side. There, State Route 14 meanders past more spectacular scenery.

Western Section: This begins near Troutdale on I-84 and follows Crown Point Highway for about twenty-one miles then rejoins I-84 at exit # 35. If you drive the old highway get your camera ready; some of the most famous shots of the Gorge have been photographed along it, not to mention the waterfalls. At Vista House atop Crown Point the famous Gorge winds greet you, as well as magnificent views across to Washington and great camera views looking east and west along the river. Vista House has a gift shop, restrooms, water and public information booth. It is open from April through mid-October.

This section boasts three state parks—Latourell, Shepperd's Dell and Bridal Veil—that offer hiking, views of waterfalls and placid picnic areas. Watch for Wahkeena Falls Picnic Area with a picnic shelter complete with stone fireplace. You can walk Trail #420 to Wahkeena Falls bridge and then on to Wahkeena, and it will lead to Fairy Falls and Wahkeena Springs.

A stop at Multnomah Falls is a must. Trails take you to the top of the fourth highest waterfall in the United States, at 620 feet. The historic lodge houses a restaurant, gift shop, snack bar and restrooms. Then drive two miles east to Oneonta Gorge. Many of the wildflowers found only in the Gorge reside here at the Oneonta Botanical Area. Horsetail Falls Picnic Area is a half-mile beyond Oneonta. A mile beyond Horsetail, Ainsworth State Park gives you a spot to camp with forty-five tent or trailer sites, restrooms, showers, water, sewer, electricity and a dumping station.

Back on I-84, continuing east five miles, you will come to Bonneville Dam at Exit #40. The Bonneville Dam Historical Site has free admission to the visitor center and tours. Visit the fish hatchery and fish-viewing window from 9:00 to 5:00 daily. Or turn right off exit #40 and drive to the Wahclella Falls trailhead for a short hike to the falls.

Eastern Section: This segment begins at I-84 Exit #69 and follows US Hwy 30 to Exit #83 near The Dalles. The byway is a total of thirty-seven miles long and follows two-lane paved roads suitable for all types of vehicles. Historic Columbia River Highway usually remains open all year and there are numerous state parks along the byway. Most of the parks have only day-use facilities, such as hiking trails and picnic areas, but offer the chance to stop and enjoy the beauty of the area and hike to waterfalls.

■ Celilo Park

Between Biggs and The Dalles, OR, on I-84. The Corps of Discovery portaged around these great falls, now under water. The park has interpretive signs regarding the expedition. Wishram, Washington, is directly across the river from Celilo Park; here the Corps camped October 22–23, 1805, in preparation to portage around Celilo Falls. They camped here again on the return trip April 31, 1806. The Indian village at Wishram was the site of the largest trading center of the Columbia.

■ The Dalles Dam

East of The Dalles, Oregon, I-84. This dam covered the rich fishing grounds and trade center of the Pacific Plateau trade region. It also covered the remains of a land bridge across the Columbia. The Dalles is one of the oldest inhabited locations in North America, serving as a center of Native American trade for 10,000 years. The city of The Dalles offers Fort Dalles Historical Museum, self-guided historical walks, tours of The Dalles Dam and colorful views of windsurfers. The visitor center has a guided tour train.

■ Horsethief State Park

Near Goldendale, Washington, State Hwy 14. Located two miles east off US Hwy 197, the Corps camped here after running the dangerous "Narrows" upriver. Clark visited a village here and noted there were twenty wooden houses there. The park is the site of a former Indian village where you can see some of the oldest pictographs in the northwest. The park offers interpretation of Indian cultures, walks and tours of many Indian petroglyphs, including "She Who Watches." If you would like to view the park's pictographs and petroglyphs, call ahead for a reservation. Tours are given on Fridays and Saturdays for a limited number of people. There are also places for swimming, rock climbing, boating or fishing here.

■ Fort Rock Campsite
The Dalles, Oregon, I-84, Exit 83. The Corps established a campsite here, which could be defended. This camp was a defensive position against possible attack from less than friendly Indians. They used it on the outbound and return journeys.

■ Cascade Locks Marine Park
Cascade Locks, Oregon, I-84. This is where the captains saw evidence of a massive landslide that had once blocked the river and gave rise to the myth of "The Bridge of the Gods." Visitors to the Cascade Locks Museum and Cascade Locks Sternwheeler can enjoy displays and riverboat cruises.

■ Hood River
Hood River, Oregon, I-84. This river is known as the windsurfing capitol of the Northwest. The area has two historic hotels and an opportunity to cross the Hood River Toll Bridge to Washington. The River County Museum, in Hood River, has displays of Indian artifacts, including Klickitat baskets.

■ Bonneville Lock and Dam
Downriver from Cascade Locks, Oregon, I-84 and Stevenson, WA, on Hwy 14. The dam's backwaters covered the Cascades of the Columbia that the explorers portaged around. Visitor centers are located on both sides of the river. The center on the Oregon side has a fish hatchery, trails and an exhibit on Lewis and Clark on the River.

■ Maryhill State Park
Maryhill, WA, at the intersection of US Hwy 97 and State Hwy 14, a bridge across the Columbia here connects with Biggs, OR. Near here the explorers found the Indians had blankets and a sailor's jacket, indicating trade up the Columbia from sea captains on the coast.

■ The Maryhill Museum
Goldendale, Washington, State Hwy 14. The museum sits high

Maryhill Museum, Goldendale, Washington.

above the Columbia River near Goldendale; it is three miles west of US Hwy 97 on Hwy 14. It can be accessed from I-84 by crossing the bridge at Biggs, Oregon. This Chateau home of entrepreneur and visionary Sam Hill was dedicated by Queen Marie of Romania in 1929 and opened as a museum in 1940. It is a rare find in the sparsely populated, arid bluffs of the Columbia Gorge. There are eighty-seven drawings and sculptures by Rodin; they are "Rodin's Rodins"—those he kept for himself, including a version of "The Thinker" with a foot missing. In addition, there are European and American paintings. The museum has an extensive collection of Native American tools and basketry, with 800 pieces representing tribes and styles of weaving from North America.

Queen Marie of Romania met Sam Hill in Europe after World War I while doing relief work. They became friends and she subsequently came to dedicate the museum in progress and later donated her personal collection, which is an unusual centerpiece to the museum. Queen Marie was a cousin of Czar Nicholas II, the last Russian emperor, and the collection holds some rare icons, including a slashed portrait of the czar and coronation jewels.

Sam Hill's replica of Stonehenge sits three miles east of the museum and was built by Hill, a pacifist, to honor the war dead of Klickitat County. Hill was mistakenly informed that Stonehenge was a site where young men were sacrificed to the war gods and wanted to show that young men were still being sacrificed. Today the monument also memorializes the dead from World War II, Korea and Vietnam. It is free and has a great view of the Gorge.

■ **Columbia Gorge Discovery Center and Wasco County Historical Museum**

The Dalles, Oregon, Hwy 30. The museum has a major interpretive center that features displays on the geologic splendor of the Gorge, 10,000 years of tribal life, Lewis and Clark and other significant explorations and modern-day Gorge resources.

CHAPTER 5

The Pacific at Last— From Beacon Rock to the Pacific

■ November 1, 1805 ■

I t took nine grueling days for the Corps of Discovery to make their way through and around rapids from Celilo Falls to the Cascades. Getting through the Cascades took another two days. In three more days they passed Beacon Rock. The Indians knew it marked the last of the rapids on the Columbia River and the beginning of tidal influence from the ocean, 150 miles downriver. The river was now widening. The weather was damp and cold, at times one couldn't see another person fifty paces away.

Beacon Rock is the core of an ancient volcano. Ice-age floods that ripped through the Columbia River Gorge eroded the softer material away and left the rock standing like a beacon on the banks of the Columbia River. It was called the silent sentinel by the explorers.

The news came November 3. "Towards evening," Joseph Whitehouse wrote in his journal, "we met several Indians in a canoe who were going up the River. They signed to us that in two sleeps we should see the ocean vessels and white people." Then Clark reported that Indians coming upriver "informed us they saw 3 vessels below." Did the Corps of Discovery imagine beaches and ease and rest just around the corner? Maybe. They didn't say. But around the corner was not ease, just more trouble.

Relations with the Indians had been tense at times but on November 4, 1805, near the mouth of the Willamette River the tension escalated. Members of a large Skilloots village there were invited into camp. This proved to be a serious mistake when the heavily armed warriors became "assuming and disagreeable," taking items they wanted, including Clark's highly prized ceremonial pipe tomahawk. The Corp took to the river and stayed for an hour under cover of darkness to avoid further trouble. They had learned a lesson and would never again allow such a large number of Indians in their camp.

The Chinookan-speaking Skilloots were secondary middlemen along the western arm of the larger Pacific-Plateau trade network. They occupied both sides of the Columbia between the Washougal and Cowlitz Rivers, near present-day Vancouver, Washington, and Portland, Oregon. Their aggressive behavior may have been based on fear of losing their position as traders.

The trade jargon spoken contained some English words and phrases brought upriver by coastal Indians who traded with passing ships. Over the next few days the Corps continued to paddle downriver and more reports came that the ocean was only a few sleeps away. One English-speaking Indian said he traded often with a Mr. Haley and he was now at the mouth of the Columbia. More and more European trade goods appeared in the homes and on the backs of Indians. A guide who paddled ahead of them through the fog wore a blue sailor jacket.

The morning of November 7, 1805, brought a parting of the fog and a sight that must have been like heaven opening up. According to Clark's journal he felt something like that. "Ocian in view!" he wrote, "Ocian in view! O! The joy."

They paddled furiously and camped thirty-two miles downriver near Pillar Rock, on the northern shore of the Columbia in present-day Wahkiakum County, Washington. That evening again Clark reflected the elation they must have felt when he wrote, "Great joy in camp, we are in view of the Ocian, this great Pacific Ocean which we [have] been so long anxious to see." They deserved to see the ocean and rejoice after paddling, walking and riding horseback for 4,000 miles over a period of nineteen months. Sadly, they were looking at Gray's Bay and the Pacific was twenty miles away. The closer they got to the Pacific, the worse the situation became. Pinned against the northern shoreline for two weeks by storms Clark described as "tempestuous and horrible."

On November 8, the party continued westward along the shore and entered Gray's Bay where they faced a strong offshore storm that carried strong swells. They were forced to camp in the margin between the high and ebb tides near Gray's Point and were trapped there for four hungry, wet days. Their dugouts proved to be even more useless under these conditions, and in the night the high tide overwhelmed them. Huge driftwood logs—some of them 200 feet long and seven feet in diameter—were thrown up on the shore.

It was a situation with no good solution. It was dangerous to stay and too hazardous to take to the water. The next day Clark noted in his journal, "At this dismal point we must Spend another night as the wind & waves are too high to proceed."

By November 14, they noted that robes and half of the few clothes the men still had were now rotted away. Snow was visible on the high mountaintops to the south and they needed to hunt and kill elk for skins and food. They were in a precarious and dangerous situation.

The storm abated briefly the afternoon of November 15 and they were able to round Point Distress, go past an empty Chinook village of thirty-six houses and reach a suitable campsite. Here they camped on the site of what is known as Old Chinook Town, just east of the promontory of land on which Fort Columbia is situated. The camp was near the small creek that flows into the bay at that point.

While Clark concluded, correctly, that they had traveled as far as they could by water, Sergeant Gass declared it a victorious milestone as he wrote, "We are now at the end of our voyage, which has been completely accomplished according to the intention of the expedition, the object of which was to discover a passage by the way of the Missouri and Columbia rivers to the Pacific ocean; notwithstanding the difficulties, privations and dangers, which we had to encounter, endure and surmount."

They named their place of respite Station Camp and stayed for ten days. While they were there, Clark set out to explore and on November 17, 1805, told all the Corps of Discovery members who wanted to see more of the main ocean to be ready early the next morning. Clark and eleven others trekked for two and a half days. They climbed the headlands of Cape Disappointment and saw the immense Pacific, which Clark called the Great South Sea. They shot a California condor that had a wingspan of nine feet. They hiked along the sandy shore at Long Beach and turned back to Station Camp.

By the 23rd of November they had explored, camped and been as cold and wet as they ever wanted to be again. The captains must have been discussing what to do next. Seven Indians from the Clatsop tribe on the south bank of the Columbia crossed in a canoe, bringing two sea otter skins but they asked such high prices (blue beads principally, which the party had run out of) that no business could be transacted. From the Clatsops they learned more about the country on the south shore.

That day Lewis set the pace by blazing his name on a tree with his branding iron. The others followed suit by carving name, date and "by land." They planted a flag and thereby staked their claim.

They were well beyond the boundaries of the Louisiana Purchase that extended only to the Rocky Mountains. Both the United States and Britain had staked claims to the Northwest, although both claims were weak. By cutting their initials and message into tree trunks and planting the flag, they marked new territory for the United States.

The next day a vote was conducted to decide what to do next. The captains gathered the party and asked the group to make a decision whether to move to the south shore, where they knew they could hunt elk and maintain a winter camp, or return upriver. If they were not successful there, they would "proceed on" upriver. Sacagawea expressed the desire to have plenty of wappato, wherever they were. The vote was one short of being unanimous to move to the south shore, to present-day Oregon.

The thirty-three individuals of the Corps of Discovery were facing a wet, isolated winter together. Maybe the vote empowered them to face the situation not to mention a trip all the way back to Missouri, which must have seemed a tiresome prospect at this time. The fact remains that a vote of this kind, with all included equally, would not be implemented in the United States for another hundred years (a black man and an Indian woman voted).

Wappato

On the way downriver, the Corps passed present-day Sauvie Island that hid the mouth of the Willamette River from their view. They had purchased and enjoyed wappato along the lower Columbia and Clark called the island Wappato Island because of the many wappato growing there. It was described as having an agreeable taste and "answers well in place of bread." Wappato contributed to the diets of Indians downriver as camas bulbs did for Indians of the interior basin.

Lewis described twenty-mile long Wappato Island and the importance of the root as a food source to the neighboring Indians. Wappato grew in numerous ponds on this island and in other areas along the lower Columbia. This bulb was a staple article of commerce along the river and grows beneath the mud. "It is never out of season; so that at all times of the year the valley is frequented by the neighboring Indians who come to gather it. It is collected chiefly by the women, who employ for the purpose canoes from 10 to 14 feet in length, about 2 feet wide and 9 inches deep, and tapering form the middle, where they are about 20 inches wide. They are sufficient to contain a single person and several bushels of roots, yet so very light that a woman can carry them with ease. She takes one of these canoes into a pond where the water is as high as the breast, and by means of her toes separates from the root this bulb, which on being freed from the mud rises immediately to the surface of the water and is thrown into the canoe. In this manner these patient females remain in the water for several hours, even in the depth of winter. This plant is found through the whole extent of the valley in which we now are, but does not grow along the Columbia farther eastward."

FOLLOWING THE TRAIL
—Scenic Drives and Trail Sites

■ Memaloose State Park
Megler Rest Area, Hwy 401. The Chinook Indians along the Columbia often used islands in the river as places to lay the bones of their dead on open pyres. Near The Dalles, the captains named a large

rock in the middle of the river Sepulchar Island. The Indian name was simply Memaloose, meaning place of the dead. This area of Pacific County, Washington, was home for the expedition for more than five days as they were pinned down by a storm, with "every man as wet as water could make them." The island is now covered by water and the park is a favorite for water sports enthusiasts and windsurfers; summer weather is at its hottest in this part of the Columbia River Gorge.

■ Beacon Rock State Park
Milepost 35, State Hwy 14. The Corps camped here at the rock's base. Here is an opportunity to stand where the explorers stood. The park has more than twenty miles of roads and trails open to hiking, mountain biking and equestrian use. You can actually climb to the top of 848-foot Beacon Rock; it's an easy one-mile trail to take in the panoramic view from the largest monolith in the United States. This place is in the heart of the Columbia River Gorge National Scenic Area. It is located thirty-five miles east of Vancouver, Washington, and ten miles west of Stevenson, Washington, on State Route 14. The park offers birding, picnicking, hikes, boating and camping. There are many campsites, picnic sites and other facilities. From Seattle, take I-5 south to Vancouver. Just north of Vancouver, take I-205 south; follow I-205 south to the Hwy 14 exit, follow the highway east. Beacon Rock and the park entrance are located at milepost 35. From Portland, take I-84 eastbound along the Columbia River to Cascade Locks. At Cascade Locks, cross the Columbia River into Washington on the Bridge of the Gods toll bridge. Turn left onto Hwy 14 and follow for seven miles to Beacon Rock.

■ Rooster Rock State Park
West of Troutdale, I-84. The Corps camped here under "a high projecting rock on the Lar [board] side," Clark. Vista House/Crown Point is on a loop off I-84 west of Troutdale. From here you have a spectacular view of the gorge and several Lewis and Clark sites. It has interpretive signs and exhibits.

■ Lewis and Clark State Recreation Site
Troutdale, I-84. This site is at the mouth of the Sandy River. The Corps of Discovery hunters explored this area, which they called the

"Quicksand." Sgt. Pryor went upriver six miles. There are interpretive signs and a botanical trail; be sure to check out the historical museum in Troutdale.

■ Parkers Landing
Washougal, WA. This site is on the Washington side of the Columbia at the mouth of the Washougal River. The Corp camped here for six days, March 31 to April 5, 1806, while they traded with the Indians and hunted elk for the return trip.

■ Sauvie Island
Access is north of Portland, OR, off Hwy 30. Look for the sign to Sauvie Island Bridge to access this rural island between the Columbia River and Multnomah Channel. There is plenty of water here and the Corps called it "Wappato Island" for the potatolike water root that grew here in abundance and was harvested by the Indians as a diet staple.

The Wildlife Management Area here serves as a rest stop for 2 to 3 million migratory waterfowl; 150,000 ducks and geese spend the winter; tundra swans and sandhill cranes are there in the fall and you will see great blue herons, wood ducks, beaver and red foxes the year round. The 12,000 acres of state-owned habitat allows fishing and some access is restricted during hunting season and spring. There is an 1853-era house and museum.

■ Lewis and Clark Campsite State Park
Two miles southeast of Chinook, US Hwy 101. This was the campsite of November 15 to 24, 1805, from which Lewis and Clark first saw the breakers from the Pacific Ocean.

■ Fort Canby State Park and Lewis and Clark Interpretive Center
South of Ilwaco, Washington, Hwy 100. At this site the expedition viewed the Pacific Ocean at Cape Disappointment. On the high promontory

Carved wooden statue of explorers, Lewis and Clark Campsite State Park, south of Chinook, WA.

you might have a sense of the vastness of the Pacific, especially viewed through the eyes of explorers who had just pushed their way halfway across the continent. The major interpretive center is devoted to an overview of the Lewis and Clark Expedition. The interpretive center is a vital part of Fort Canby State Park and it tells a comprehensive story of the expedition.

■ Deer Island

US Hwy 30, east of Portland, OR. The Corps visited twice and gave the island its name, after killing several deer. Here they learned that the Indian name *e-lal-lar* meant "deer." There is a highway marker on US Hwy 30 east of Portland.

■ Ilwaco Heritage Museum

Ilwaco, Washington, Hwy 103. Located near Cape Disappointment, the museum has exhibits on Chinook Indian culture, exploration and settlement as well as the Corp of Discovery. Very near Clark's trail.

■ Long Beach, Washington

Long Beach, Hwy 103. William Clark arrived on the sandy shore of Long Beach Peninsula after setting out to explore from their camp on the Columbia, Station Camp. They proceeded up the beach about four miles before returning. Clark wrote, "I proceeded up the Course....& marked my name & the Day of the Month on a pine tree..." Long Beach has the "Mark of Triumph" statue and interpretation.

■ Fort Columbia State Park

Two miles southeast of Chinook, US Route 101. An interpretive center here is devoted mostly to the coast artillery story. There also is a large exhibit relating to the Chinook Indians. This is a National Historic Landmark. Members of the Lewis and Clark expedition experienced mixed emotions when they reached their goal near the present site of Fort Columbia Historical State Park. They were elated at having accomplished their mission—crossing from the Missouri to the Pacific—but they were greeted by a prolonged spell of wet, windy and cold weather that made them utterly miserable.

■ Willapa National Wildlife Refuge

Headquarters are on Hwy 1101 on the eastern side of Willapa Bay, a short drive from the Long Beach Peninsula. This large and pristine refuge offers delightful viewing of wildlife and wetland creatures. It contains a three-mile interpretive trail and five campgrounds with a total of twenty-five camping sites. Visitors are advised to check the tide table before venturing out in order to ensure a high enough tide to reach the campground area without getting stuck in bay mud. The Willapa National Wildlife Refuge has regulations and instructions specific to camping on Long Island (1-360-484-3482).

While many stands of trees of the size described by Clark have long ago been logged, there are still a few places in the area where such trees can still be seen. If you want to have a look at remnants of an ancient forest, this 4,700-acre site is a great place to visit. Managed by the Willapa National Wildlife Service, the 274-acre stand of cedars includes trees which are five to seven feet in diameter and 150–160 feet high, looking much the same as the ones which the expedition members would have seen all around them during November, 1805.

■ Ridgefield National Wildlife Refuge Complex

Five refuges in southwest Washington make up the Ridgefield National Wildlife Refuge Complex. All the sites provide habitat for wintering waterfowl and year-round viewing for a variety of wildlife.

To get to the Ridgefield NWR site headquarters, take Exit 14 off I-5 to the town of Ridgefield. From the town you can access two units. To the River S Unit, take a left on S. 9th Avenue or Hillhurst Rd. The refuge entrance is located .7 miles up the hill on the right-hand side of the road. For the Carry Unit, go west until Pioneer Street makes a "T" with Main Avenue; turn right on Main and go north for a mile. The entrance is on the left.

The Ridgeport Dairy Unit is off the Fourth Plain Exit, #1D, off I-5. Head west towards the Port of Vancouver. Fourth Plain Road becomes Lower River Road. Stay on Lower River and go left at the "Y." Drive about eight miles to reach the entrance.

Franz Lake, Pierce and Steigerwald Lake National Wildlife Refuges are all located on State Hwy 14 in the Columbia Gorge National Scenic Area. Franz Lake and Steigerwald Lake NWR can be viewed from a scenic overlook on Hwy 14. The Pierce NWR supports one of the last remaining chum salmon runs in the lower Columbia River drainage The south end of the refuge can be viewed from the Beacon Rock Trail. For more information, contact The Ridgefield National Wildlife Refuge Manager at (360) 887-4106.

■ Lewis and Clark National Wildlife Refuge

This large NWR includes about a third of the Columbia River estuary in Oregon, beginning twelve miles above the river's mouth and extending fifteen miles. This large and wonderful haven for all kinds of migrating waterfowl also provides estuary habitat for many species of fish, spawning, nursery and feeding areas for young salmon while they go through the physical changes that allow them to survive in salt water.

Unless you have a boat, you will only be able to look out over some of the islands from US Hwy 30, five miles east of Astoria, OR. Be glad, anyway, that a safe haven has been provided for the creatures. Lewis and Clark called this area "Seal Islands."

■ Fort Canby State Park

Located at the extreme south end of Long Beach Peninsula on Hwy 100, here you can see the crashing surf and the mix of the mighty Columbia and the Pacific. There are old-growth forests, quiet wetlands and a variety of wildlife. Great for bird watching, there is a beautiful trail system along the headlands overlooking the Pacific Ocean.

CHAPTER 6

A Winter Passed at Fort Clatsop

■ November 26, 1805 ■
to
March 18, 1806

On the morning of November 25, the Corps of Discovery set out from Station Camp on the Washington side of the Columbia. They were still fighting the tidewaters of the Pacific in unwieldy dugouts. After struggling along the shore they camped for the night, hungry. "Oh how disagreeable is our situation," Clark again wrote. With spirits low and hunger upon them Sacagawea produced a piece of stale bread from her furs that she had been saving for her baby and gave it to Clark. He accepted it gratefully and ate ravenously. Moments like these must have defined the sense of community shared by the members of the group. They had traveled across half of North America, crossed and recrossed the Continental Divide and survived hardship together.

Lewis managed to get a small canoe across to the south shore in the Tongue Point area. He then explored further west and found a suitable campsite within earshot of the Pacific's breakers. The site was five miles south of present-day Astoria, Oregon, and protected from winter storms. When the rest of the party eventually arrived, they must have felt a great sense of relief. A small river was nearby to provide fresh water and the Clatsops had promised there would

Map: Courtesy of Cannon Beach Chamber of Commerce

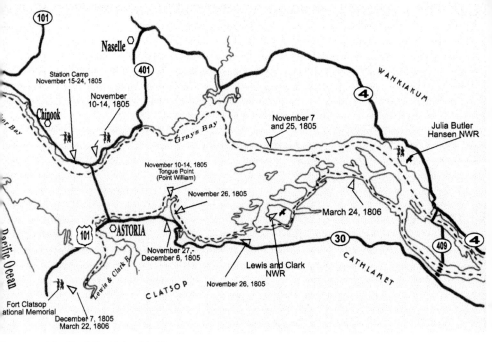

Mouth of the Columbia River.

be plenty of elk to hunt. Here, near what is now called Young's Bay, they set about building their log stockade they called Fort Clatsop after their Indian neighbors.

The Corps hoped to find a trading ship at the mouth of the Columbia that would allow them to replenish their meager stock of goods. They wanted to send specimens back and even obtain passage for themselves back to the east. In a twist of fate, however, they somehow missed the trading ships that were in the area just when the explorers arrived at Fort Clatsop. They were left to resupply on their own and that meant a lot of trading with the Clatsops. The Clatsops told Lewis there was seldom snow in the area. "If this should be the case," he wrote, always concerned for the welfare of his men, "it will most certainly be the best situation for our naked party dressed as they are altogether in leather."

They built a fifty-foot square stockade that consisted of a row of three cabins facing another row of four. A parade ground twenty feet wide separated them. At Christmas time they settled into their Fort Clatsop quarters and by candlelight the captains caught up on a backlog of journaling, botanical note taking, and mapmaking.

Besides having a winter home sheltered from the elements and plenty of game to hunt, the Corps wanted to be able to make salt.

Clark himself stated indifference to having salt for his food, but Lewis and the others wanted it to season their diet of elk, deer and dog. Clark set out immediately to find a direct route to the seacoast and on December 28 five men were sent to establish a salt camp. Five days later they found a suitable place with seawater that had a high salt content. There were stones for building a fireplace, wood, game and fresh water. The site was near some houses of Clatsop and Tillamook Indians and on the beach at present-day Seaside, Oregon. They continued to make salt here at the rate of three quarts to a gallon a day for two months.

On January 8, 1806, Clark gazed at the spectacular coastline from Tillamook Head. He wrote "...from this point I beheld the grandest and most pleasing prospects which my eyes ever surveyed." The coastline is still grand and pleasing and can be seen today from any number of sites along Highway 101.

Clark and a party that included Sacagawea had gone south from Seaside to find a whale reported to be beached at present-day Cannon Beach, Oregon, the farthest point south they reached. They arrived "...at a beautiful sand shore [but] found only the skeleton of this monster on the sand," wrote William Clark. The nearby Tillamook and Clatsop Indians had found the whale and had already cut up most of it and taken it away, but Clark traded for some meat and blubber, anyway. The beached whale was at the mouth of Ecola Creek, the Clatsop name for whale.

Surrounded by lush old-growth forest, wetlands and wildlife, the Corps rested from their journey and prepared for the arduous trip home. The 33-member party spent the winter of 1805–06 learning life ways from the Clatsops, making moccasins and buckskin clothing and storing food. The rest from traveling may have been welcome, but by the time to leave they had become thoroughly bored. Relations with the nearby Clatsop and Chinook villagers were kept at arms-length by the captains. The Corps came with preconceived ideas of coastal Natives as incorrigible thieves, ideas rooted in the previous experience with Skilloots on the Columbia. Lewis described the Clatsops as "great higlers in trade and if they conceive you anxious to purchase [they] will be a whole day bargaining for a handfull of roots." From the viewpoint of the Indians they were simply doing business in the same way they traded with ships along the coast.

Cultural ideas of physical attractiveness also colored the attitudes of the Corps of Discovery. The Indians that they came across on the coast didn't fit the Euro-American image. They were shorter in stature and their facial features were described as "low and ill-shaped." The Plains Indians had appealed much more to the Corps' ideas of a norm. Added to this was an incident when meat was stolen from the expedition. Thinking of others as so different from us that they deserve little respect can lead to regret. During preparations for the return home in March, the Corps tried to purchase canoes from the Clatsops and found they refused to sell at a price they could afford. Unfortunately, the commitment to never steal from the Indians was forgotten for the first time during the expedition. Lewis reported in his journal, "We yet want another canoe, and as the Clatsops will not sell us one at a price which we can afford to give we will take one from them in lue of the six elk which they stole from us in the winter." The essential honesty of the expedition had been tarnished.

As they set out upriver, the entourage carried with them journals filled by Lewis with descriptions of plants, birds, mammals, fish, amphibians, weather data and much detailed information on Indian cultures. Clark drew illustrations of many of the animals and plants and updated maps of the journey. Clark calculated they had traveled 4,132 miles in 554 days, from Wood River to the mouth of the Columbia. On March 18, 1806, the long journey home was begun.

FOLLOWING THE TRAIL
—Scenic Drives and Trail Sites

■ Fort Clatsop National Memorial

Near Warrenton, Oregon, US Hwy 101 Business Loop, access off US 101 at Warrenton. This where the Corps spent the winter of 1805–06 near a Clatsop Indian village. You can tour the reconstructed fort and visit an excellent interpretive center. During spring and summer there are living history demonstrations; daily life at the fort can be seen here and you can walk through the log stockade and see the quarters. Notice the lack of sunlight and imagine it during a wet coastal winter. Out of 100 days the Corp spent there, only twelve were without rain. The site is open year around and offers a muse-

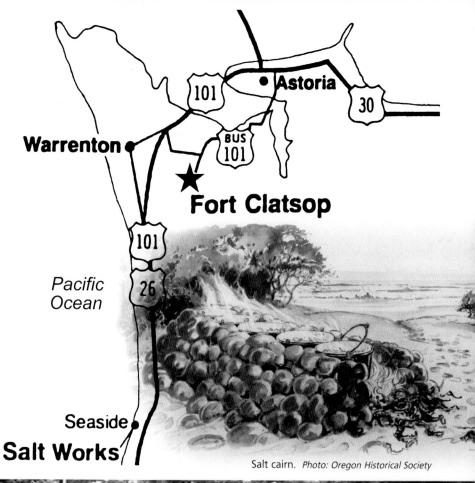

101

● Astoria

30

BUS
101

Warrenton ●

★
Fort Clatsop

101

*Pacific
Ocean*

26

Seaside ●

Salt Works

Salt cairn. *Photo: Oregon Historical Society*

Fort Clatsop National Memorial, replica of original fort.

um, bookstore and hiking. A picnic area and biking trails are also located nearby. The Salt Works site in Seaside, Oregon, a part of the park, commemorates the site where the Expedition boiled sea water to make salt. Hike the Lewis and Clark Trail that eventually will lead from the Fort Clatsop picnic area all the way to the beach, with forest so dense in some places that it is near dark in the daytime.

■ Salt Works

Seaside, Oregon, US Hwy 101. Here you can visit the site of the expedition's salt works. A replica of the seawater boiling operation marks the approximate location of the salt makers' camp. To reach the salt works, drive on US 101 to Seaside. Turn west, towards the ocean, on Avenue G and follow the signs to South Beach Drive and Lewis and Clark Way. The site is on Lewis and Clark Way, which dead ends at a walking path along the beach.

This site was identified by a Clatsop Indian who recalled a story her mother told of white men boiling water on that spot. Jenny Michele was born in 1816 and, prior to her death in 1905, she identified the rock pile that marked the site.

■ Les Shirley Park and Ecola State Park

Access is just north of Cannon Beach city limits; watch for signs to turn west off US Hwy 101. This is the site of the beached whale the explorers heard of. Clark took a small party, including Sacagawea, to seethe whale at the mouth of a creek he named Ecola, a native word for whale. Interpretive signs mark this location in Les Shirley Park on the north side of the creek. You can hike the route taken by the explorers between the salt works at Seaside and the beached whale site. The trail begins at Ecola State Park and crosses the western edge of Tillamook Head to Seaside.

The views of the coastline with Haystack Rock and Tillamook Rock Lighthouse are breathtaking. From here you can access coastal rainforest hiking trails; there are great opportunities for whale watching as well as birding and wildlife viewing. Most of the trails follow the route followed by the members of the expedition 200 years ago. The park is for day use only and charges a fee. The Tillamook Rock Lighthouse is on a rock nearly two miles out at sea and can be seen from Ecola State Park viewpoint and looking north from Cannon Beach.

■ The Oregon Coast Bike Trail

Along US Hwy 101. The trail extends along the highway and makes bike-touring possible along nearly the entire stretch of the Oregon Coast.

■ Three Capes Scenic Route

West of Tillamook, US Hwy 101. This route loops off the highway between Pacific City and west of Tillamook. It leads past Cape Meares, Cape Lookout and Cape Kiwanda.

■ Columbia River Maritime Museum

Astoria, Oregon, US Hwy 30. Located on Astoria's historic waterfront, it displays one of the most extensive collections of nautical artifacts on the West Coast. Designated Oregon's official state maritime museum, this outstanding institution with 24,000 square feet of exhibit space is the only nationally accredited maritime museum in the western United States.

■ Fort Stevens State Park, Historic Area and Military Museum

Near Warrenton, Oregon, off US Hwy 101. The site of a "Clatsop town" noted by Clark. Originally, it was commissioned as a Civil War fortification in 1863. Fort Stevens was deactivated as a military fort shortly after World War II. It is now an Oregon State Park. Its museum features military artifacts, guided tours, interpretive displays, movies and living history demonstrations. Fourteen miles of biking trails are within the park. Consider a climb to the commander's station for a scenic view of the Columbia River and South Jetty.

CHAPTER 7

Homeward Bound

▪ March 23, 1806 ▪

When the Corp pulled out of Fort Clatsop on March 23, 1806, they left a letter posted on the fort to tell the world that they had made the crossing over the mountains to the Pacific. After an industrious, though boring, winter they now had plenty of clothing and between 300–400 pair of moccasins. They had little else, for food had become scarce and they now relied on their guns to provide food as they set about to travel up the Columbia. They had six boats, three of their original dugouts made the previous September, two canoes purchased from Indians and one stolen from the Clatsops.

That night they camped at Tongue Point, or Pt. William, at present-day Warren's Landing north of Astoria. They were able to kill two elk and trade for dog and wappato the next day at a Cathlamet village. The totem posts that supported the entrance to the houses were elaborately carved and the journals note that the Cathlamets seemed to be more fond of carving than their neighbors.

An interesting turn of events came when the owner of the canoe stolen from the Clatsops showed up. It turned out the owner was not the Clatsops but a Cathlamet Indian. An encounter occurred when they set out again upriver and took a wrong turn. They were over-taken by the Cathlamet who showed them the way to the main channel. One man identified the canoe as his own by the personal and symbolic carving on it. The Corps was able to right their wrongdoing by paying the owner of the canoe with an elk skin.

On their trip downriver, the group had experienced trouble with Skilloots but now they were welcomed. In fact, they were visited overnight by two Skilloots and then were treated with kindness and hospitality at a Skilloots village.

It seems the Skilloots and Chinooks had recently been warring, but there was a compromise of sorts where the Chinooks agreed to stay at the lower part of the river and trade between the Chinooks and Skilloots was conducted by mutual friends—Clatsops, Cathlamet and Wahkiakums. The journals noted that the Skilloots had cultural similarities to the Clatsops, Chinooks and other tribes at the mouth of the Columbia. It is helpful to remember that there are various tribes within linguistic groups and that speaking the same language did not necessarily mean constant peace.

They camped on the north shore, near present-day Vancouver, Washington, on March 31, 1806. The next day's travel brought them to the mouth of the Washougal River, still on the north shore, and near present-day Parker's Landing. They stayed for six days, trading with the local Natives and hunting elk to restock their food supplies. Here they met Indians coming downriver who were very hungry "...they seemed almost starved and greedily picked up the bones and refuse meat thrown away by us." They were holding out for the next salmon run which, wasn't expected until May 2—the next full moon. By April 7 the Corps of Discovery had enough dried meat to last them until they met the Shahaptian-speaking tribes again and they set off upriver.

Most of the waterfalls in the gorge are on the south side of the river since the north shore has eroded more over time. Lewis described the terrain they passed on April 9, 1806, "The hills have now become mountains. High on each side are rocky steep covered generally with fir and white cedar." He was looking at the south shore of the river when he said, "several small streams fall from a much greater height, and in their descent become a perfect mist which collecting on the rocks below again become visible and descend a second time in the same manner before they reach the base of the rocks." These can be seen on the south shore now along the Columbia Gorge National Scenic Highway.

The rapids they encountered, beginning east of today's Portland, Oregon, were heightened by spring runoff and accordingly more dangerous. They had reached the head of tidewater, about fifty miles upriver from present-day Vancouver, Washington, and on April 10 they hauled their boats up over the Cascades. The Cascades are just that, a series of cascading water, divided into Upper and Lower Cascades. The Upper Cascades are the most challenging, "the head of the rapids" according to the journals, at a turn in the river at present-day Cascade Locks, Oregon. The Corp portaged the Upper Cascades, losing a dugout in the process, and camped April 12 at the same site as their October 30 camp.

On April 15 they camped again at Fort Rock near The Dalles where they had camped on the downriver trip. They set about preparing to abandon river travel and to trade for horses with the Indians.

The Indians were determined to exact their tolls and the expedition was able to trade for only four horses; they needed twelve. Over the next nine days they continued upriver, partly by land and partly with some remaining boats. Some of the horses they obtained were "vicious stallions" who broke free and delayed their travel. According to the journals, there were problems again with more hard bargaining for horses and some Skilloots stealing. Finally, on April 24, they traveled "all by land," and they moved upriver on the Washington side.

Eager to meet Walla Wallas and obtain food they halted, weary men and horses, on April 27. They were soon joined by their friend, Walla Walla Chief Yellept, who was friendly and hospitable. He enticed them to stay with his people for several days while they were entertained at a feast with several hundred Walla Wallas and Yakimas. This occurred opposite the mouth of the Walla Walla River, fifteen miles south of the confluence of the Snake and the Columbia. Lewis and Clark had given a medal to Yellept the previous year and now he proved to be a strong ally. He furnished them with canoes to take their baggage across the river and provided clear directions on how to reach the Nez Perce on a direct overland route. This route is entirely south of the Snake River and goes east mainly along the Touchet River via Dayton, Washington, to Lewiston, Idaho, and Nez Perce country. In Washington they crossed Walla Walla, Columbia and Garfield Counties and touched the northern

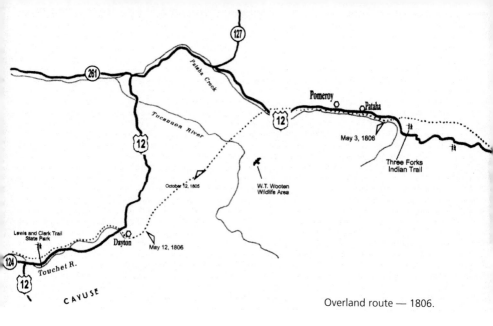

Overland route — 1806.

border of Asotin County. The well-traveled Indian trail led them more or less straight to the mouth of the Clearwater.

They made forty miles the first day and camped between today's towns of Prescott and Waitsburg, Washington. The trail they followed was later a wagon road and the ruts have remained visible in grass-covered areas for 200 years.

On May 3 they camped in a creek bottom near present-day Pataha in Asotin County, Washington. They were cold, wet and had the last of their dog for supper. The journals state, "We continued up the bottoms of the creek for two miles, till the road began to leave the creek and cross the hills to the plains. We therefore camped for the night in a grove of cottonwood, after a disagreeable journey of 28 miles."

The explorers were traveling an ancient Indian trail, a highway of sorts. It was used by Nez Perce and other tribes, too. It appears to have been the main thoroughfare for the tribes that traveled across the Rockies to the buffalo hunting grounds in Montana and back again. They often used travois along the way and when the ruts became too deep from the poles being dragged behind ponies the simple transports were routed off to the side, thus making another, parallel, trail. These rutted indentations on the earth are still visible today in some places that have not been plowed repeatedly. The trails left are discernible from livestock trails since they tend to be straight, rather than meandering, especially on hillsides. With each

Travois used at the burial of Old Chief Joseph of the Nez Perce.
Photo: R. R. Beale collection

passing season the visible signs of the trail are dimming as the hoofs of more cattle cross them and as the grasses build a sod base, which is stronger each year.

They then followed "the road over the plains, N.60 degrees E.," a branch of the trail they had followed up the creek. This trail is marked on Hwy 12 east of Pomeroy, WA, and the east branch of the trail can still be seen on the hill across the highway; the southerly branch, which went toward the Blue Mountains, is visible toward the west-southwest on the hillside.

The Nez Perces aided Lewis and Clark several times during travels through their lands. Now one of the two guides who had accompanied them to Celilo Falls on the Columbia in October, the Nez Perce chief, Big Horn, or Tetoharsky, came to meet them near Three Forks. He assured they would find a camp and provisions near the Snake River the next day. He went ahead and said he would meet them there. Clark wrote on May 3, 1806, that the chief had been "...very instrumental in procuring us a hospitable and friendly reception among the natives. He had now come a considerable distance to meet us."

Arrowroot balsam along the Snake River.

Big Horn could not have known, when he offered to guide the explorers, what harbingers of change they were. Soon the peaceful trail of the Nez Perces would carry missionaries, soldiers and opportunists. In the 1860s the trail was crowded at times with men who hurried to the gold fields at Pierce, Idaho, and at times the blood of those travelers was spilled by thieves that operated from a way-station at Three Forks.

The Corps reached Alpowai Creek on May 4 and were met again by Chief Big Horn. The next day he joined them and they proceeded up the Clearwater to present-day Kamiah, Idaho, and to the camp of Twisted Hair, the gracious Nez Perce chief that had promised to care for their horses.

FOLLOWING THE TRAIL
—Scenic Drives and Trail Sites

Parker's Landing
The route taken by the Corps across the northwest was the same westward in 1805 and returning in 1806, except for the overland route when they left the Columbia at the mouth of the Walla Walla River. They then proceeded across present-day eastern Washington to the Snake River as shown on the map. Trail sites and points of interest are found in earlier chapters where the trail was the same both ways.

Three Forks Site
Garfield County, US Hwy 12. Six miles east of Pomeroy, the only incorporated town in the county, there is a historical marker of a campsite of the Lewis and Clark party. At this site, called Three Forks, the trail followed along Pataha Creek and forked with one trail veering south toward the Blue Mountains and another east across the plains toward the Snake River. This is the trail taken by Lewis and Clark.

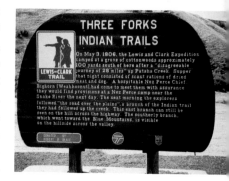

Three Forks Indian Trail

"We continued up the bottoms of the creek for two miles, till the road began to leave the creek and cross the hills to the plains. We therefore camped for the night in a grove of cottonwood, after a disagreeable journey of 28 miles." — CLARK, MAY 3, 1806

This photograph taken in 1910 clearly shows the Indian road referred to by the explorers. Here on the hill above Pataha Creek six miles east of Pomeroy, Washington, there is indeed a grove of cottonwood trees on the right. Local old timers call this site, where the Corps found shelter and firewood, Three Forks. Here the trail used by the Nez Perce and the explorers forked: the south fork led toward the Blue Mountains while the east fork, taken by Lewis and Clark, led over the hills toward the Snake River.

CHAPTER 8

Among Friends Again — the Nez Perce

o retrieve their Shoshone horses from Twisted Hair, the Corp continued up the Clearwater River from present-day Lewiston, Idaho. They were hungry and nearly out of trading goods. Fortunately Clark's reputation with the Indians for successfully treating various ailments had preceded them as they camped at the mouth of Potlatch Creek with a small band of Nez Perce under Chief Cut Nose. On May 5, 1806, Lewis reported in his journal, "We arrived very hungry and weary, but could not purchase any provisions, except a small quantity of the roots and bread of the cows [cous]. They had, however, heard of our medical skill, and made many applications for assistance, but we refused to do anything unless they gave us either dogs or horses to eat. We soon had nearly fifty patients. A chief brought his wife with an abscess on her back, and promised to furnish us with a horse to-morrow if we would relieve her." The woman reported the next morning she was much better and her husband kept his promise of a horse, which was immediately killed and eaten.

They crossed the Clearwater to the south shore and moved upriver and then along a divide between the Clearwater and Little

Canyon Creek. Here they found the camp of Twisted Hair, who had befriended them the previous year and accompanied them downriver to the Columbia. The horses they had left in his care were scattered. He had been forced to keep the peace between two lesser chiefs that competed for the honor of caring for the horses; he did this by allowing each to take some of the horses. Over the next few days the horses were gathered and the cache of saddles, tack, powder and lead were retrieved from Canoe Camp.

Their good friend Chief Twisted Hair now took them to the camp of Chief Broken Arm. A two-day council there with important chiefs from throughout the region followed. Finally a vote was taken and it was unanimously agreed that American fur trading houses would be welcomed and that they would attempt peace with their enemies. Not only that, the Corps would have a guide, Red Bear, and two other chiefs to guide them back across the mountains.

Now it was time to celebrate with the 4,000 people who had gathered with feasting, dancing, singing, gambling, games, smoking and giving of gifts. Nez Perce history notes that they enjoyed Cruzatte's fiddle playing and singing as well as York's style of dancing "with feet." Chief Many Wounds said that everyone was very sorry when the Corps, including Sacagawea, her baby and York, left.

From May 14 to June 10 the Corp camped near present-day Kamiah, Idaho. They had amicable relations with the Nez Perce while they waited until the snow-covered Bitterroots became passable again. Clark was well liked for his friendly personality and his reputation as a doctor. The year before he had cared for a large number of people afflicted with an eye ailment and people came to him to wait patiently for his attention. He treated with sulfur, cream of tartar, laudanum and portable soup and was fondly remembered for generations by the Nez Perce.

According to Nez Perce history, Clark formed a liaison with a Nez Perce woman and they married "Indian custom." She traveled with him to Deer Lodge, Montana, where she met Nez Perces returning home and crossed back over the mountains with them. Back with her people she gave birth to a baby boy. He was called Daytime Smoker or Son of Clark and was proud of his paternal ancestry; he was reportedly light-skinned and blue-eyed. (York also fathered a child with a Nez Perce woman, but the child died before adulthood.) Son of Clark fought the whites in the Nez Perce War of

1877 and died a prisoner of war in Oklahoma after a tragic and eloquent surrender by Chief Joseph of the Nez Perce. This is one of many ironies of history that came about from the westward explorations and movement of the past 200 years.

During the early spring, a time of hunger for everyone, the members of the Corps were engaged in obtaining food in every possible way. The hunters shot bear, grouse and ground squirrels and they all traded for camas, cous and cous bread whenever they could. The trade stock was nearly bankrupt and they did their best with such items as buttons, empty containers, paint, thread and ribbon although the Nez Perce wanted knives, kettles, blankets and moccasin awls.

As they prepared to recross the formidable Rocky Mountains, a party was sent out to a fishery on the Lower Salmon River, which was a tributary of the Snake River. Guided by Nez Perce, they left Camp Choppunish (present-day Kamiah, Idaho), and crossed the prairie on an Indian trail toward the Salmon River. They came to the Salmon River about twenty miles upstream from the confluence with the Snake only to discover the Indians were still waiting for the salmon run to reach them. In order to reach another fishery downstream on the Snake they climbed back up into the Craig Mountains that rim the prairie above the river canyons and then down to the Snake where they purchased salmon.

By the time they got back to Camp Choppunish seven days later, the seventeen fish they brought were mostly spoiled. The fish were wel-

Drawing of white salmon trout by Clark.
Photo: Oregon Historical Society

comed anyway, eaten and deemed delicious—an indication of the food shortage. Two days later the captains ordered preparations to break camp and resume their journey eastward. Against the advice of the Nez Perce, who said it was too early for the snow-packed mountains to be passable, they forged ahead stopping at the edge of the prairie to hunt and replenish their provisions. Then onward again until they reached a wall of snow eight to twelve feet deep. They cached some baggage and retreated to the Weippe Prairie.

They set out again June 24, 1806. This time the way was easier but they encountered a huge drift that was all but impassable. Red Bear, one of their three guides, showed Lewis how to "make the snow go fast." He set fire to the brush and forest and the drift was cleared of snow. They proceeded on the Lolo Trail and over the rough terrain until they reached Traveler's Rest on July 1, 1806. They had sped across the mountains compared to the westward trip, which averaged about twenty-six miles a day; they made the return trip in six days. It had taken eleven days westbound. They soaked in the warm waters of Lolo Hot Springs and left the mountains behind. "This," said Clark, "is like once more returning to the land of the living." The hot springs still flow at Lolo Pass, 5,233 feet high.

York

York had been the personal slave of William Clark since adolescence when they made the epic journey to the Pacific and back again. Without a doubt he was a contributor to the success of the expedition as much as anyone was. He carried his share of the work load and daily duties and was an intelligent and strong member of the Corps of Discovery. In addition, his blackness was a passport to acceptance. York served as a topic of interest that kept the attention of the Indians who had never seen a black person when otherwise they might have lost interest in the explorers. During the tense moments when Lewis waited with Cameahwait for Clark's return from upriver he was very concerned that the skittish Shoshone would vanish and leave them with no means of obtaining horses to cross the mountains. It is clear that York, the black man with the short curled hair, was a topic of interest enough to keep the Shoshone and their horses waiting. Later with the Shoshone horses, the party proceeded over the Bitterroot Mountains, even now a wilderness area that defies penetration. The entire party suffered terribly and stumbled out of the mountains to the Weippe Prairie camas gathering grounds where they met the Nez Perce. Again, York's affect on the Indians was carried on in their oral history and even added to their vocabulary. Reportedly he was named *Tse-mook-tse-mook To-to-kean*, meaning a black Indian, and that name became the Nez Perce word for a black person.

The Lemhi Shoshones tell that York sired a son called *Too-tivo*, meaning black white man. Among the Nez Perces, an oral history tells that there was child of York's who died before maturity. York could swim—not all members of the expedition could. Dangerous rapids on the Columbia River called for measures of safety and non-swimmers walked around while those who could swim rode the dugouts through the thundering falls and rapids of the Great River. No doubt York was one who shot the rapids in a dugout hewn a month before on the shores of the Clearwater in Idaho.

Twice in November, 1805, York broke new ground for a black. He accompanied Clark and a party to the beach and stood at the edge of the Pacific as the first black man to cross the continent north of Mexico. Then, on November 24 he participated in the vote, along with Sacagawea and other members of the expedition to decide where to spend the winter. Clark honored York by naming a tributary of the Yellowstone and island in the upper Missouri for him. It seems right that York, as a valued member of the party, would be given his freedom when they returned to St. Louis. Sadly, this did not happen and he remained a slave for five more years.

The slaveholding tradition was ingrained in Clark and perhaps York, too. These two who shared the epic journey were surely bonded and respected each other, yet back in St. Louis in 1809 Clark wrote to his brother that he was vexed with York and other servants. Clark reported that York was insolent and sulky, that Clark had "trounded" him, and that he wanted to hire him out. According to Washington Irving who interviewed Clark in later years, York had been freed by Clark and set up in a drayage business that failed and that York later died of cholera in Tennessee.

Photo: Montana State Historical Society

Alspotokit, "Daytime Smoker"

This photograph was taken in Montana in 1863. It was confirmed to be the Indian who called himself Clark, and that his hair was yellow. White historians who met this man in later years reported that he was very proud of his paternal ancestry. When asked, he would straighten his body, strike his chest and proclaim "Me Clark." Most reports agree that he was engaged in the Nez Perce War of 1877. He was captured at Bear Paw Mountain, along with Chief Joseph and others, and was sent to Indian Territory, where he died in 1878 or 1879.

Sacagawea

"...Your woman, who accompanied you that long, dangerous, and fatiguing route to the Pacific Ocan and back, deserved a greater reward for her attention and services on that route than we had in our power to give her."

— Excerpt from a letter to CHARBONNEAU from CLARK, written en route to St. Louis August 20, 1806

Sacagawea was fourteen years old when she "...was delivered of a fine boy...her labor was tedious and the pain violent," wrote Lewis, February 11, 1805. She was fed ground up snake rattlers to assist in bringing the baby. Something worked, but Lewis was not convinced it had been the Indian medicine.

Less than two months later she left the Mandan village where the Corps of Discovery had wintered and carried her baby, Pomp, in a cradleboard on her back. Her husband, Touissant Charbonneau, had been hired as an interpreter for the expedition, but Lewis and Clark knew Sacagawea was the critical link with the Shoshone—her people. She had been captured several years earlier in a Hidatsa raid and had lived among the Minitaree before she was traded to Charbonneau.

Her story is a romantic one—a teenage mother who carried her baby across the Continental Divide and to the Pacific. On the way she helped the Corps find their way to her people so they could trade for horses for the trip over the mountains. When Sacagawea discovered that her brother was now the Shoshone chief it was a stroke of luck for the expedition and a heart-warming reunion for her. The moment was pivotal, now the horses could be obtained.

Maybe the self-sacrificing woman softened and strengthened the men of the Corps. Certainly she had given her prized blue-beaded belt to Clark so he could get a handsome fur robe from the Indians in November, 1805. At Fort Clatsop she gave two dozen weasel tails to Clark for Christmas. This, in the middle of a dismal, hungry winter.

On January 5, 1806 she insisted that she be taken to see the monstrous fish that had been beached at Tillamook. She had endured every hardship on that trip and now she was not about to be left at the fort. She wanted to go. She deserved to go and said so; Clark included her in the party. When they left Fort Clatsop for the return trip, Pomp was a year old. Again, she carried him.

The record of what happened after the return to St. Louis is not clear. But we know that Clark had been fond of Pomp, and had offered to raise him and educate him. In 1910 Pomp, sister Lizette, and his half brother Toussaint were given into Clark's care. It was reported Sacagawea died two years later, probably of complications of childbirth. However, there are other histories that say she returned to her people and lived to be nearly a hundred years.

Pomp was educated and in fact became a favorite of Prince Paul Wilhelm of Wuertemberg, Germany. He had met Pomp in a trader's village and invited him to come to Europe. Pomp lived there for six years and learned several languages before he returned to the western frontier. Once he was back in the west, he adopted the mountain man lifestyle and rode with well-known frontiersmen, such as Jim Bridger and Kit Carson. Later the well-respected French-Indian was appointed mayor of San Luis Rey Mission in California. He served as mayor, justice of the peace and chief administrator of the law. One of his first acts was to establish an Indian school.

Epilogue

ewis and Clark returned to St. Louis, September 23, 1806. They had been gone so long without any word that most people assumed they were dead. A great celebration ensued with a welcoming ball in their honor. Lewis lost no time in beginning his report to President Jefferson, and he began working on it on September 26.

Meriwether Lewis

His accomplishments were lauded by the country and by the president. Jefferson rewarded Lewis with double pay and gave him 1,600 acres of land. The next year, the president appointed him Governor of the Louisiana Territory. Sadly, the classic hero's journey was over for Lewis.

He was extremely bright, well educated and a patriot in the tradition of his Virginia revolutionary father. Thomas Jefferson had been a close family friend of the Lewis' when Meriwether was growing up. His father died when he was only fourteen; later, Jefferson appointed Lewis to be his personal assistant.

Lewis was a complex and gifted man. He was used to leading and his expectations, both of himself and others, resulted in frequent outbursts of temper and impatience. He was headstrong and self-critical. He suffered from a melancholy and depression that seemed to be family traits. Ultimately it was this, after surviving the danger and hardships of the expedition, that took his life.

Following the expedition, he became a harried bureaucrat in a society that chafed. There were reports to be published and pressure to get the journals published. He was scrutinized from all sides and he took to drinking and leaving tasks undone. The War and Treasury Department had questions about Lewis' official expenses. He agreed to meet with them but never made it there. He died of an apparent self-inflicted gunshot wound on October 11, 1809, on the Nachez Trace in Tennessee as he traveled to Washington to defend his spending. He had written his last will and testament while he was on the trip and had twice tried to kill himself. William Clark and Thomas Jefferson, the closest of his fiends, did not doubt he had taken his own life.

His journals, scientific reports as well as his courage and focus on the journey were somewhat ignored throughout most of the remaining century. His journals were published in the Thwaites edition at the end of the century and a revival and recognition of the accomplishments of Lewis and Clark occurred. Both the captains have rightfully been honored with statues, and schools and a college are named after them. The bicentennial celebration of their epic journey is a celebration of all the members of the expedition.

William Clark

Clark and Lewis shared somewhat similar backgrounds, though Clark was about four years older. His family was originally from the same region of Virginia that was home to the Lewises and Thomas Jefferson. The Clarks moved westward to homestead before William was born. His family members were Revolutionary War veterans and knew Thomas Jefferson well. Entering the military at the age of nineteen, Clark was a captain with Lewis under him as ensign. Later, when offered the co-commandment of the Corps of Discovery he came out of military retirement to happily undertake the trip with his friend Lewis. They were to be co-captains, but Jefferson broke his promise and assigned Clark the rank of second lieutenant. Lewis simply disregarded the official title and continued to address Clark, and treat him, as captain.

Clark was openly fond of Sacagawea's son Pomp and showed consideration for Sacagawea too. He did take Pomp under his care after the expedition was over and educated him, as he had offered to do. He also relinquished ownership of his slave York, though nearly a decade later.

Clark was paid equally with Lewis at the completion of the expedition, double pay and 1,600 acres of land. Moreover, a grateful Jefferson gave him a double appointment in the Territory of Upper Louisiana; he was Brigadier General of Militia and Superintendent of Indian Affairs.

After Lewis' death, Clark collaborated with Nicholas Biddle on the publication of the expedition journals, to which Biddle's interviews with Clark were added. Clark spent the rest of his life in service to his country and family and died at the age sixty-eight in St. Louis.

Discoveries New to Science

CHAPTER 1 ■ Discoveries made from the entry into Idaho to the Clearwater River

Animals:
Oregon ruffled grouse *Bonasa umbellus sabini*
Franklin's grouse *Canachites canadensis franklinii*
Black-headed jay *Cyanocitta stelleri annectens*
Clark's nutcracker *Nucifraga columbiana*
Mountain goat *Oreamnos americanus americanus*

Plants:
Rocky Mountain maple *Acer glabrum*
Grand fir *Abies grandis*
Subalpine fir *Abies Lasiocarpa*
Sitka alder *Alnus sinuata*
Camas *Camassia quamash*
Western larch *Larix occidentalis*
Orange honeysuckle *Lonicera ciliosa*
Engelmann's spruce *Picea engelmannii*
Whitebark pine *Pinus albicaulis*
Lodgepole pine *Pinus contorta*
Ponderosa pine *Pinus ponderosa*
Common snowberry *Symphoricarpos albus laevigatus*
Pacific yew *Taxus brevifolia*
Western red cedar *Thuja Plicata*
Blue huckleberry *Vaccinium membranaceum*

Indian Tribes Encountered:
Shahaptian linguistic family: Flatheads, Nez Perce
Shoshonean linguistic family: Shoshone

CHAPTER 3 ■ Discoveries made from the Clearwater River to the Columbia River

Animals:
none

Plants:
Oregon white-topped aster *Aster oregonus*
Netleaf hackberry *Celtis reticulata*
Many-spined opuntia *Opuntia polyacantha*
Peach-leaved willow *Salix amygdaloides*
Slender willow *Salix exigua*

Indian Tribes Encountered:
Shahaptian linguistic family: Wanapums, Yakimas

CHAPTER 5 ■ Discoveries made from the mouth of the Snake River on the Columbia River to the Ocean

Animals:
Columbia black-tailed deer *Dama hemionus columbianus*
Columbia sharp-tailed grouse *Pedioecetes phasianellus columbianus*
Harbor seal *Phoca vitulina richardii*
Steelhead trout *Salmo gairdneri*
California newt *Triturus torosus torosus*
Great-tailed fox *Vulpes fulva macroura*

Plants:
Vine Maple *Acer circinatum*
Madrone *Arbutus menziesii*
Dull Oregon grape *Berberis nervosa*
California hazelnut *Corylus californica*
Oregon boxwood *Pachistima myrsinites*
Oregon white oak *Quercus garryana*

Shahaptian linguistic family: Walulas (Walla Wallas), Umatillas or Cayuse, Eneeshurs (a division of Wayampam)

Chinookan linguistic family: Echeloots or Echelutes (Wishram); Chilluckittequaws, Skilloots, Cathlapotles, Wahkiakums, Cathlamets Chinooks, Clatsops.

Salishan linguistic family: Chehalis

CHAPTER 6 ■ Discoveries made during the winter at Fort Clatsop

Animals:

White sturgeon *Acipenser transmontanus*
Western grebe *Aechmophorus occidentalis*
White-fronted goose *Anser albifrons frontalis*
Mountain beaver *Aplodontia rufa rufa*
Ring-necked duck *Aythya collaris*
Lesser Canada goose *Branta canadensis leucopareia*
Roosevelt's elk *Cervus canadensis*
Western common crow *Corvus brachyrhynchos hesperis*
Northwestern crow *Corvus caurinus*
Western American raven *Corvus corax sinuatus*
Western pileated woodpecker *Dryocopus pileatus picinus*
Townsend's chipmunk *Eutamias townsendii townsendii*
Pacific fulmar *Fulmarus glacialis rodgersii*
Oregon bobcat *Lynx rufus fasciatus*
Striped skunk *Mephitis mephitis notata*
Whistling swan *Olor columbianus*
Oregon jay *Perisoreus canadensis obscurus*
Townsend's mole *Scapanus townsendii*
Western gray squirrel *Sciurus griseus griseus*
Douglas' squirrel; chickaree *Tamiasciurus douglasii douglasii*
Richardson's red squirrel *Tamiasciurus hudsonicus hudsonicus*
Western badger *Taxidea taxus neglecta*
Eulachon; candlefish *Thaleichthys pacificua*
Western winter wren *Troglodytes troglodytes pacificus*

Plants:
Red alder *Alnus rubra*
Edible thistle; "Shanataque" *Cirsium edule*
Salal *Caultheriaa shallon*
Seashore lupine; "culwhayma" *Lupinus littorralis*
Sitka spruce *Picea sitchensis*
Western white pine *Pinus monticola*
Western bracken *Pteridium aquilinum*
Oregon crabapple *Pyrus fusca*
Mountain hemlock *Tsuga mertensiana*
Evergreen huckleberry *Vaccinium ovatum*

Indian Tribes Encountered:
Salishan linguistic family: Tillamooks

Bibliogaphy

Ambrose, Stephen E. 1996. *Undaunted Courage*. New York.: Simon & Schuster.

Bergon, Frank. 1989. *The Journals of Lewis and Clark*. New York, NY: Penguin Books.

Betts, Robert B. 1985. *In Search of York*. University Press of Colorado and the Lewis and Clark Trail Heritage Foundation.

Biddle, Nicholas. 1993. *The Journals of the Expedition, Volume 2*. Norwalk, CT: The Heritage Press.

Botkin, Daniel B. 1995. *Our Natural History, The Lessons of Lewis and Clark*. New York, N.Y.: G.P. Putnam's Sons.

Clark, Ella E. 1953. *Indian Legends of the Pacific Northwest*. University of California Press.

Cutwright, Paul Russell. 1969. *Lewis and Clark: Pioneering Naturalists*. Urbana, Chicago, London: University of Illinois Press.

DeVoto, Bernard. 1953. *The Journals of Lewis and Clark*. New York, New York: Houghton Mifflin Company.

Fifer, Barbara, and Soderberg, Vicky. 1998. "Along the Trail with Lewis and Clark." *Montana Magazine*: Great Falls, MT.

Gustafson, R. W. 1998. *The Dog Who Helped Explore America*. R.W. Gustafson, Condrad, MT.

Hawke, David Freeman. 1980. *Those Tremendous Mountains*. New York. W.W. Norton and Co., Inc.

Hunsaker, Joyce Badgley, 2001. *Sacagawea Speaks: Beyond the Shining Mountains with Lewis and Clark*. Two Dot, Guilford, Connecticut.

Jones, Landon Y. 2000. *Essential Lewis and Clark*. New York. Harper Collins Publishers.

Lavender, David Seivert. 1990. *The Way to the Western Sea*. Anchor Books, New York.

MacGregor, Carol Lynn. 1997. *The Journals of Patrick Gass*. Missoula, MT. Mountain Press Publishing Co.

Moulton, Gary, Editor. 1997. *The Journals of Joseph Whitehouse*. University of Nebraska Press, Lincoln.

Ronda, James P. 1984. *Lewis and Clark Among the Indians*. Lincoln, NB: University of Nebraska Press, Lincoln.

Saling, Ann. 1999. *Northwest Nature Factbook*. Portland, OR: West Wind Press.

Salisbury, Albert and Jane. 1950. *Two Captains West*. Seattle: Superior Publishing Co.

Snyder, Gerald S. 1970. *In the Footsteps of Lewis and Clark*. The National Geographic Society.

Space, Ralph. 2001. *The Lolo Trail*. Missoula, MT: Historic Montana Publishing.

Strong, Emory and Ruth. 1995. *Seeking Western Waters*. Portland: Oregon Historical Society Press.

Sullivan, George. 1999. *Lewis and Clark*. New York: Scholastic Reference.

Index